The Manager's Guide to Change

The Manager's Guide to Change

Elmer H. Burack
Florence Torda

Lifetime Learning Publications
Belmont, California

A division of Wadsworth, Inc.

Editing, design, and production supervision: Brian Williams
Interior design: Marjorie Spiegelman and Christopher Keith
Editing: Tom Belina
Cartoons: Bob Haydock
Composition: Graphic Typesetting Service

© 1979 by Wadsworth, Inc. All rights reserved. No part of this book may be reproduced, stored in a retrieval system, or transcribed, in any form or by any means, electronic, mechanical, photocopying, recording, or otherwise, without the prior written permission of the publisher, Lifetime Learning Publications, Belmont, California 94002, a division of Wadsworth, Inc.

Printed in the United States of America

1 2 3 4 5 6 7 8 9 10—83 82 81 80 79

Library of Congress Cataloging in Publication Data

Burack, Elmer H
   The manager's guide to change.

   Bibliography: p.
   Includes index.
   1. Organizational change. I. Torda, Florence, joint author. II. Title.
HD58.8.B87   658.4'06   79-15537
ISBN 0-534-97995-5

Contents

	Preface	**Page ix**
	Introduction	**Page xi**
Chapter 1	**Change Is Here to Stay** Change within, and surrounding you. Recognizing change. Change as an opportunity for better management. Aims and focus of the book.	**Page 1**
Chapter 2	**Four Basic Questions About Change** Four questions that organize your thinking about change. Where has change taken place? How does it affect me? Do I have abilities to change? Do I want to change?	**Page 7**
Chapter 3	**Reacting to Change** Causes of resistance to change. Attachment to the present. The inconvenience factor. Need for predictability. Does change equal progress? Personal feelings.	**Page 21**
Chapter 4	**Sorting Things Out** Realistic planning assessments for change. Seeing change from all angles. Systems thinking. Anticipating problems. Applications.	**Page 37**

Chapter 5   **Goals for Change**   Page 53
Defining goals to bring about change. Goals must communicate to help meet resistance. The power of meaningful goals. Making goals work for change.

Chapter 6   **Helping Others to Change: External Influences**   Page 69
Adapting to external circumstances. Managing change—people and circumstances. Using role play to comprehend change. Strategies to understand powerful or respected "messages."

Chapter 7   **Helping Others: Leaders as Models for Change**   Page 93
How to influence others to understand and manage change. Use of training and development to effect change. Constructive use of conflict. Using change to increase motivation and performance.

Chapter 8   **Organization Development as an Aid to Change**   Page 117
Advantages of Organization Development in promoting change. Design of change programs. Monitoring change in the organization. Three cases illustrate ideas and methods.

Chapter 9   **Policy Hang-ups that Can Block Change**   Page 145
Personal beliefs and unexamined biases in existing policies. Their inhibiting effect on organizational development. Can you spot yours? Impeding and facilitating change in

Contents vii

organizational policy and planning. Participating, recruiting, and training. Avoidance of ruling out change. Stimulating change.

Chapter 10   **Taking on Large-Scale Change**   **Page 163**
Integrating and applying what you have learned so far about managing change. Planning and directing a comprehensive change program. Working out your own example.

Chapter 11   **Credentialing of Professionals to Meet Demands of Change**   **Page 181**
Increasing organizational specialization calls for increasing quality control. Credentialing is the answer—a force for change that will increasingly affect you. Preparing the individual to meet credentialing requirements.

Chapter 12   **Summing Up—and Looking Ahead**   **Page 195**
A review of central ideas along with suggestions for proceeding effectively within organizational constraints. Some answers to your "Yes, buts"...

Appendix I   **Ideas and Guidelines from the Change Literature**   **Page 207**
A summary of selected publications organized around the four basic questions.

Appendix II   **Sample Completed Exercises for Self-Growth**   **Page 223**

Index   **Page 233**

Preface

This book is based on more than ten years' experience with change situations in many different types of organizations involving all types of organization members. It is a distillation of literally hundreds of incidents in real-life organizations, as well as of scores of studies by knowledgeable researchers and practitioners. The result is a practical guide to increase your expertise in dealing with change. Exercises are provided to help you gather together key ideas and apply them to your own change situations. These exercises are at once trial runs for applying what you have learned and self-checks on your comprehension of the concepts presented. Gaining competency in managing change is a "do-able" activity—and doing the exercises will increase your competence just that much more rapidly.

We wish to thank Thomas M. Calero, of the Stuart School of Management, Illinois Institute of Technology, for his generosity in sharing material related to the preparation of Appendix I. We also appreciate the valuable help of numerous organization officials, managers, supervisors, and support personnel who so generously shared their experiences, insights, and frustrations.

Elmer H. Burack
Florence Torda

Introduction

Either you manage change or change manages you. There's no other choice. If you've already come to this conclusion, you are probably ready for some assistance. If you're still mulling it over, you should be warned that change will move on regardless—and make catch-up in the future ever more difficult, if possible at all. This book can help you deal more effectively with change. Doing so may involve carrying out change, initiating change, or simply accepting change—and this can be hardest of all. But no matter what your role, to deal more effectively with change it's necessary first to understand it. And that's where we begin.

As a manager, supervisor, or administrator—as a person with organizational responsibilities—you are under direct pressure to deliver change in one form or other. What may differ from situation to situation is the frequency of change or perhaps its magnitude. Regardless, everybody with any supervisory or administrative responsibility must deal with change. How you do it is your problem—literally. You may feel at times that you don't have the necessary know-how to do it. Or you may feel that the problems associated with change are too slippery to get hold of. Both mean that change may be managing you rather than you managing it.

Change need not be capricious. It can often be planned and its effects exploited. This approach to change—managing change—begins by thinking differently about change—thinking in a broader and more systematic fashion, rather than just reacting to pressure. Knowledge of specific change features and techniques plus *systems thinking,* as we will refer to it, can help you see the overall picture. This approach can also help to remove the mystery from change so that it can be planned better. Planning change, like other aspects of managing change, can be accomplished through a knowledge of change principles and processes, some analytic tools, and practical strategies for promoting change, including how and when to use them.

Becoming aware of these principles, tools, and strategies can increase your competence for dealing with change. But there are no magic formulas that will guarantee complete control at all times. Although you need not be at the mercy of change, no one is always on target in predicting future outcomes. Thus, managing change means being flexible to change. Your own savvy regarding the special circumstances of your organization will help you here—as will the amount of patience you are willing to expend.

Organizational change invariably involves people, their idiosyncracies (and yours!), entrenched social relationships, and the organization's political system. Your experience and insights, both from life experiences and from within your organization, are indispensable to workable change management approaches. Still, learning to manage change doesn't happen overnight. But, the payoff is worth the effort—both in personal satisfaction and in bottom-line results. When you manage change instead of change managing you, the chances for success increase correspondingly.

This book will help you on your way. Think of it as a compass rather than as a map. A map indicates the features you may meet as you go. A change map would tell you what is coming in the way of technological or social changes and what you should do to reap the advantages. A compass simply helps to indicate the right direction. In this sense, the book is a change compass. Thoughtfully interpreted, it will show you the right direction. The rest is up to you.

The Manager's Guide to Change is concerned primarily with change as it affects work life. But since change is a fact of *all* life, it is important to understand its ramifications in both the broadest and most personal terms. It is also true that know-how gained in nonwork activities—personal or community matters, for example—can contribute to change competency in the business world.

Accordingly, this book has two central aims: 1) to provide a comprehensive perspective on change to help you to be more aware, more willing to take on change, and generally to be more helpful to yourself and to others *wherever* change is at issue; and 2) to present specific ideas and methods of initiating and coping with change as it affects *organizational responsibilities.*

These two aims acknowledge two closely related needs: 1) to achieve personal success in fulfilling job obligations, which carries over into personal life away from work; and 2) to increase the economic bottom-line payoff to the organization.

The book focuses on your concerns as a manager, supervisor or administrator—in any kind of organization, be it business, government, or voluntary. However, it is not automatically assumed that your personal interests and needs are identical with those of your organization. Guidelines are included for managing personal as well as organizational change. The result for you should be a more confident approach to change, whatever its context.

The Manager's Guide to Change

Change Is Here to Stay 1

When was the last time you saw anyone using a slide rule?

A Managerial Model for Change

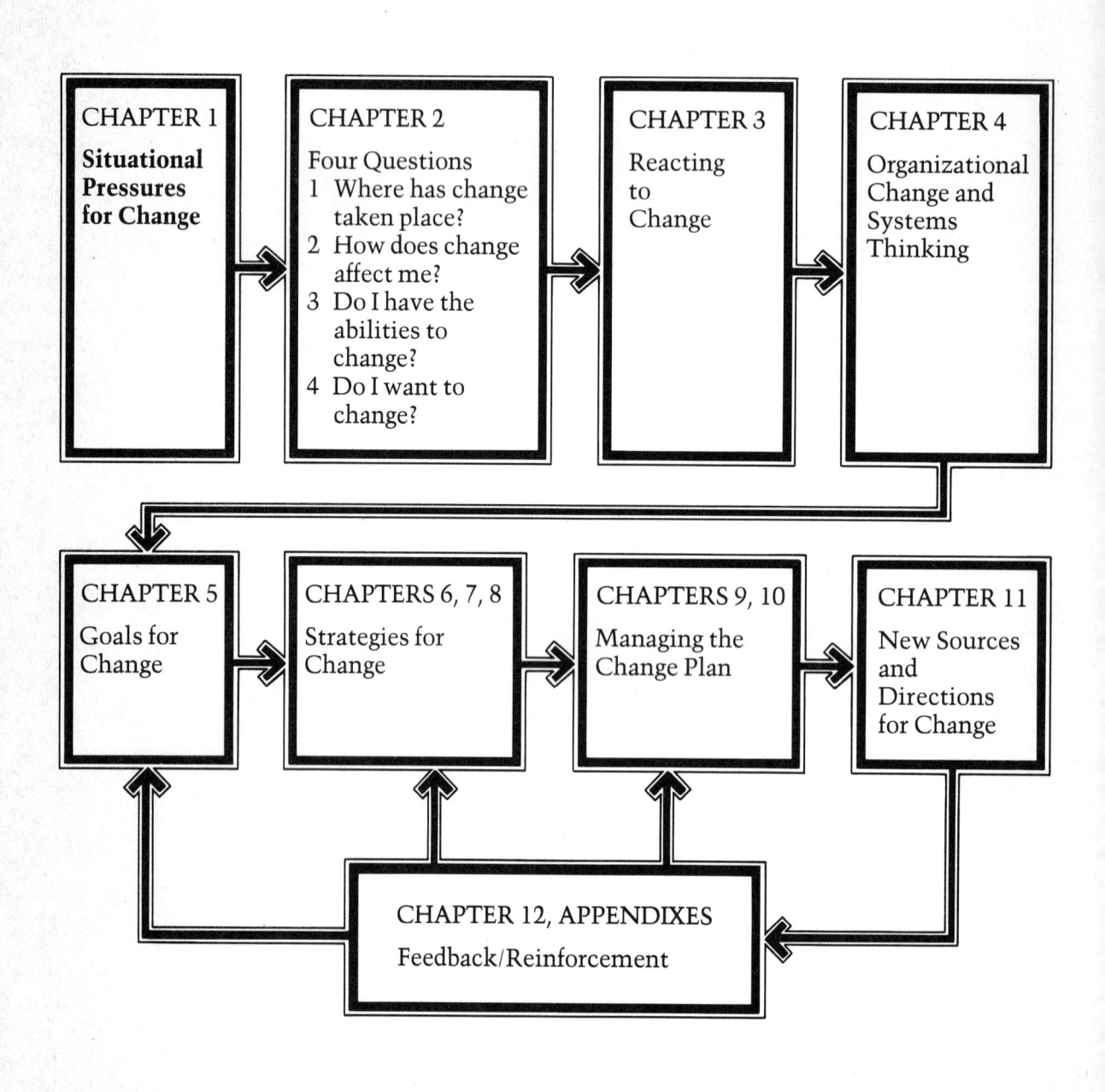

CHAPTER 1 — Situational Pressures for Change

CHAPTER 2 — Four Questions
1. Where has change taken place?
2. How does change affect me?
3. Do I have the abilities to change?
4. Do I want to change?

CHAPTER 3 — Reacting to Change

CHAPTER 4 — Organizational Change and Systems Thinking

CHAPTER 5 — Goals for Change

CHAPTERS 6, 7, 8 — Strategies for Change

CHAPTERS 9, 10 — Managing the Change Plan

CHAPTER 11 — New Sources and Directions for Change

CHAPTER 12, APPENDIXES — Feedback/Reinforcement

When was the last time you saw anyone using a slide rule? How about the last time you saw a classified ad for a Girl Friday? Or the last time you got a free road map at a service station?

These and hundreds of other changes have occurred over the past few years. Some were major events. Others may have sparked only mild interest, amusement, or annoyance. But they all had their impact, and whether you consciously thought about them or not, you adjusted to them in some manner.

The same kinds of changes—large ones and small ones—happen in the work world. Organizations change their production methods, record systems, personnel bases, and sometimes even their functions. They install computer-based systems and undertake affirmative action programs. And the people in the organization adjust as best they can.

But for the person in a managerial role, more than adjustment is called for. The function of a manager is to manage. And if change is the order of the day, then the function of the manager is to manage that change. To implement change *effectively* means taking a positive and active stance, not just passively carrying out directives from above.

Typically, managers make automatic coping responses to change as they go. Some of these are right on target because of long experience in an area or considerable intuitive insights. But at some time intuition deserts even the most gifted person, and past experience is often an unreliable guide to future events. All this makes the prospect of change unattractive, even frightening, and causes some managers to opt for "business as usual" or to react with too little too late.

Some forms of change become so interwoven with our lives that we may not fully recognize just how deeply they cut into daily actions. The inability to recognize change in the outside world, as well as within the organization, can be as damaging for the manager as an overly great concern with change.

The same is true for the manager who ignores change or pretends it hasn't taken place. Change *is* difficult to face, but the results of ignoring it are far worse. Change is here to stay.

Thinking About Change

Change is everywhere, whether it is recognized or not. Change permeates all activities, and change in one area has an impact in many other areas. Thus, change diffuses through an organization in ever widening circles. Yet at the perimeter of change, the effects may seem remote or unrelated to the initial change. This ripple effect is sometimes overlooked because of a tendency we all have to compartmentalize events. But when the pigeonholes are scrapped and some of the layers of emotion are stripped away, the full impact of change—large and small alike—becomes apparent.

For example, think about the impact of change a little thing like the hand calculator has had. How has it affected you on the job or those who work with you? How has it affected your life away from work? What impact has it had on industry? On education? On the balance of trade? (Not to mention on slide rule manufacturers.) The impact may appear slight or even nonexistent in your immediate work space, but chances are it has touched your organization and the people in it. And there's no doubt that this change has had important national and even internationl effects in terms of trade. Change at any one of these levels could easily work back to your area of responsibilities, even if there were no immediate impact. For sure, engineers, accountants, system personnel, and teachers have been affected, as have students and homemakers. Thus, for this instance of change, the question is not only one of direct effects on you but also on your associates, your organization, and society itself.

Managerial Model for Change

The Managerial Model for Change, on page 2, outlines both the plan of this book and a way of managing change in general. The first stage, which this chapter is about, is exploring the situational pressures for change. Chapter 2 introduces four basic questions to help you to assess your sensitivity to change and its consequences. These questions are critical to all change-related issues. They are used throughout the book as analytical tools.

Chapter 3 amplifies these four questions and provides a basis for better understanding yourself and others in relation to change. Resistance to or acceptance of change is viewed as a response to conflicting needs and values.

Chapter 4 introduces a key method for managing change—systems thinking. Systems thinking is a way of getting to the basics of organizational problems, thus permitting better assessment of organizational change. A note of caution—there is so much systems terminology around that people mistake knowledge of the vocabulary for ability in the use of the concept.

Questioning assumptions through systems thinking leads to asking basic questions about organizational goals and finding means of securing them. Chapter 5 helps to clarify change-related goals. In other words, do responses to change reflect desired goals?

Chapters 6, 7, and 8 present strategies for bringing about desired change. Chapter 6 focuses on those factors within an organization that can be modified, and on how external environmental factors influence the behavior of individuals. Chapter 7 stresses direct efforts to reach and change individuals. Chapter 8 recognizes that many changes that are consciously introduced involve numerous organizational areas. The principles and procedures of Organization Development are presented in this chapter as a technique for change.

Chapters 9 and 10 zero in on managing a change plan you work out for your own organization. Chapter 9 examines assumptions and features of change that underlie organizational programs and policies. In Chapter 10 change is dealt with as a large-scale activity that is called for by the organization itself. Comprehensive examples of change applications are included that involve review and integration of all previously covered topics.

Chapter 11 looks at new sources and directions for change. Among these, the growing trend towards credentialing of competency—the credentialing movement—is examined. Credentialing developments are not widely known, but this form of change has spread far beyond traditional fields and is having an increasingly stronger impact on organizations. These developments are, in addition, linked to continuing or lifelong educational activity, a central vehicle for individual change.

The final two sections of the book provide feedback and reinforcement. Chapter 12 provides an overall summary and offers insights for proceeding effectively within organizational constraints. Appendix I contains a summary of readings pertinent to the further understanding and management of change and for dealing with particular problem areas. Appendix II contains completed examples of some of the exercises as a guide for further self-study.

The Change Exercises

The exercises throughout this book will assist you in integrating and applying the change perspectives and strategies described in each chapter. Considered just as "exercises," they will remain hypothetical; taken as part of your direct participation in managing change, they can be powerful tools for change. In short, the exercises represent the critical difference between general understanding and actual skill application.

The Action Checklists at the end of each chapter are another means for skill development. They provide feedback on your understanding, a means of continuing self-evaluation, and direction for applying the change ideas described in the chapter. The use of these exercises and checklists is, of course, your choice, based on the level of understanding or skill you seek.

Four Basic Questions About Change 2

How well do you monitor your environment?

CHAPTER 1
Situational Pressures for Change

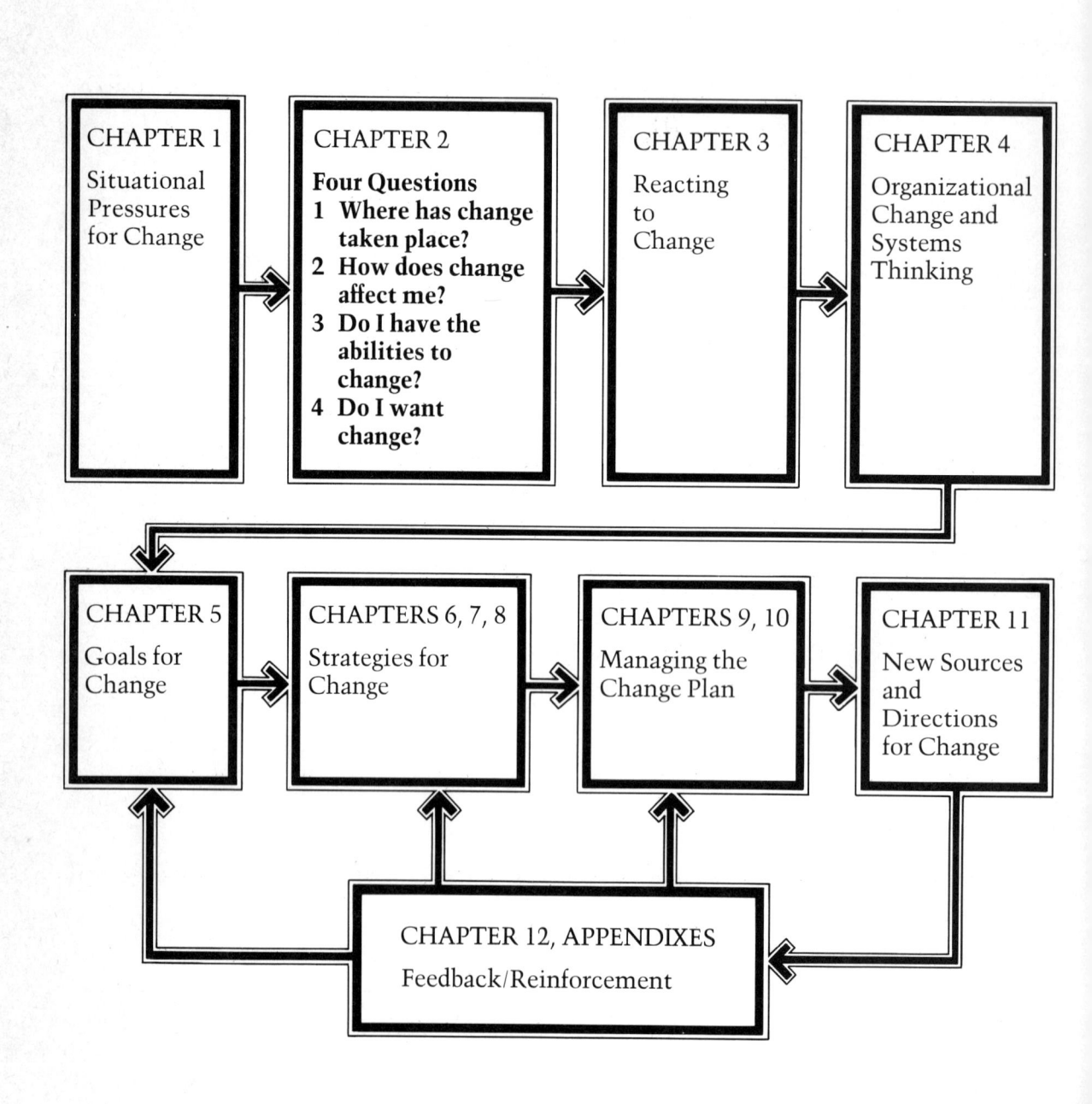

CHAPTER 2
Four Questions
1 Where has change taken place?
2 How does change affect me?
3 Do I have the abilities to change?
4 Do I want change?

CHAPTER 3
Reacting to Change

CHAPTER 4
Organizational Change and Systems Thinking

CHAPTER 5
Goals for Change

CHAPTERS 6, 7, 8
Strategies for Change

CHAPTERS 9, 10
Managing the Change Plan

CHAPTER 11
New Sources and Directions for Change

CHAPTER 12, APPENDIXES
Feedback/Reinforcement

Some people monitor their environments more actively than other people do. Note the word *monitor.* It implies an alertness to all kinds of changes. It also implies an inclination to ponder the *causes* of these changes and their interactions.

How well do you monitor your environment?

Did you react to that question feeling slightly on the defensive? Or did you react with a feeling of confidence? If you reacted confidently, you probably consider yourself a reasonably flexible person. The difficulties associated with change may seem to you more often to revolve around others than around yourself—your work associates, friends, or family.

Perhaps. But are you as flexible as you think you are? To take change in stride would indicate that you are quite *change conscious*—that you monitor your environment well. To evaluate the degree that you are change conscious, ask yourself this question:

WHERE HAS CHANGE TAKEN PLACE?

This is a broad question. It is broad in order to help you review your conceptions of what constitutes change for you—how you monitor change. How many specific answers to this question come rapidly to mind? Jot down your responses for changes occurring over the *last three years* on pp. 9 and 10. Be spontaneous. If nothing comes to mind in one area, move on to the next.

Where Has Change Taken Place?

1 Personal _____
_____

continued

Where Has Change Taken Place? (continued)

2 Family _____
   _____

3 Social _____
   _____

4 Cultural _____
   _____

5 Political _____
   _____

6 Technological _____
   _____

7 Professional _____
   _____

8 Job related _____
   _____

9 Financial _____
   _____

Impact of Change

Look over the list you made above and estimate the range of impact of each change below.

Change item	Self only	Family	Friends	Work	Employer	Own job	Other (specify)
1	_____	_____	_____	_____	_____	_____	_____
2	_____	_____	_____	_____	_____	_____	_____
3	_____	_____	_____	_____	_____	_____	_____
4	_____	_____	_____	_____	_____	_____	_____
5	_____	_____	_____	_____	_____	_____	_____
6	_____	_____	_____	_____	_____	_____	_____

continued

Impact of Change (continued)

7 _____ _____ _____ _____ _____ _____
8 _____ _____ _____ _____ _____ _____
9 _____ _____ _____ _____ _____ _____

The exercise you just completed is known as an *impact model*. Such a model is highly useful for preliminarily determining two central elements of change: (1) the source or area for initiation of change, and (2) the scope or impact of the resultant change. This impact anlysis can be further refined by recording the *degree of impact*—for example, high, medium, or low. Connecting change and scope of its impact provides a point of entry into difficult or complex change situations. At the same time, it gives you an opportunity to judge your alertness to change issues.

Judging your responses at this point, would you rate yourself high or low at being aware of change and the impact of change? If your change antennae are functioning well, you are probably aware of a lot of changes, large and small, close and far, because the world is not standing still. Further, you will be able to recognize relationships among these changes, including their possible effects on yourself, on those with whom you work, and on your areas of responsibility.

If, on the other hand, you had trouble coming up with changes that seemed worth mentioning, even to yourself, you may be failing to process the world about you. And, as a result, you may be missing useful leads in matters that are important to you.

It isn't necessarily an across-the-board thing. You may be more sensitive to change in some contexts than in others. For example, you may be acutely aware of the rising cost of real estate and what that means to you as a personal investment. But you may be relatively unaware that shrinking markets for your company's products or services will eventually affect your job. You may be very sensitive to an expected budget cut but quite fuzzy about the impact of a new computerized information system on your current procedures, let alone future activities. You may be perceptive to changes in your circle of friends or work associates but oblivious to things that are happening within your own family.

The basic question WHERE HAS CHANGE TAKEN PLACE? will help you to check the range of your perceptions. It is an analytical tool that will help you judge how well you monitor your environment.

Is That Clear?

In looking for change, don't mislead yourself into thinking that change is always something clear-cut and out there just waiting to be noticed. To an important extent, change is a matter of personal definition—change is whatever you think counts. The things that count in anyone's life are a result of many interrelated factors—life experiences, curiosity, sources of knowledge, and personal beliefs about what is relevant and important in life. Work activities may be very important to you, for example, while at the same time you may choose to ignore certain aspects of personal relationships. Change in one area counts; change in the other area doesn't. Or you may become so preoccupied responding to immediate pressures from one area that you develop blinders to other areas of change. Thus, you may be aware of some changes while unaware of others taking place at the same time.

Establishing what counts is admittedly difficult. The pressure of events close in—irate customers, breakdowns, crash programs, deadlines—can push everything else out of the picture, causing you to become single purposed. At times, events, economic considerations, or time restraints leave little or no choice. When this happens, the key idea from a change viewpoint is to recognize that in spite of these single-purpose priorities other change situations are emerging and these will also require attention. Whether it is obvious or not, change in any area is just as real as change in any other area.

Where Does It Start?

The following excerpt from an industrial consulting report illustrates a common tendency to overlook change that does not come across loudly and clearly packaged as "change." The scene is the office of James Slotkowski, superintendent of Plant No. 2, Farrington Steel. Slotkowski, a thirty-year veteran of steel making, is talking with the team leader of a large-scale research study concerned with the impact of technological change on management organization and relationships.

>   SLOTKOWSKI: *Yes, I've seen a lot of change over the years. But things are different now. Now it's business as usual.*
>   TEAM LEADER: *So you'd say there's not much change taking place?*
>   JS: *That's right.*
>   TL: *How about new equipment, methods, things like that? I understand Plant No. 2 recently installed a new basic oxygen furnace and rolling mill.*
>   JS: *That was just part of our program of continuing improvement. If that's how you define change, there have been quite a few—automatic controls, rebuilding Line No. 3, new coating equipment.*
>   TL: *How did these changes affect your people, your organization?*
>   JS: *Some of the men took some getting used to the new setup, but eventually we worked it out.*
>   TL: *How do you mean, "took some getting used to"?*
>   JS: *Oh, you know how people are. They get set in their ways. They think there's only one way to do things. We had to shuffle a few people around. We made some adjustments in personnel.*
>   TL: *So not everybody was prepared for the changes.*
>   JS: *Nope. We beefed up our Training Department when we saw what was happening. Come to think of it, that's about the time we changed our recruiting program, too.*
>   TL: *Everything satisfactory now?*
>   JS: *Not really. We're still having trouble there, as far as I'm concerned.*

The plant superintendent touches on some common difficulties when it comes to talking about change. He acknowledges some of the major changes that took place, but he refers to them as "just part of our program of continuing development" rather than as changes, that is, as something new.

Baselines for Change

But where *does* change start? What is the baseline? In reality, it is pretty much an arbitrary matter, since change is going on all the time. But to deal most effectively with change, it's important to develop *baselines* for change along the way. If you just wait for the big events, it may be too late. As far as change is concerned, you can't afford to take the business-as-usual approach to anything.

The growing complexity of organizations makes it increasingly important that baselines be established for judging the effects of change. This comes down to recognizing important events taking place within the organization—as points from which to anticipate, plan for, and measure related changes. Once these baselines are established, various types of data will be useful for interpretation of change effects or as criteria for change.

Such criteria assume many forms, among which are budgets involving costs, productivity, or the like. There are also staffing comparisons, hiring trends, "critical" social and economic indicators such as new business volume, number and types of patents, and business relocation patterns. The importance and specifics of these standards vary with the nature of the business and even with the types of unit activities within the business.

The Next Question

As James Slotkowski becomes more aware of the extent of the changes that have taken place—not just new equipment—he also moves on to consider what it means for him and for his organization. He has had need for baselines from which to gauge the types and levels of change that has taken place over particular time intervals. In effect, he asks (and partially answers) a second basic question:

HOW DOES CHANGE AFFECT ME?

The veteran steel maker is now beginning to see how changes in his organization relate to some of the troubles he has been experiencing. The connections are not all that clear at this point, but he has some ideas on which to follow through.

How Does Change Affect ME: Missing the Base

Apply the steel mill example to your own experience with change. Think of an instance where you failed to register or define some event as a new baseline for change. Consider how this may have kept you from preparing for the consequences of that change. A merger, a shuffling of top management, or the emergence of a new competitor can all be baselines for change. But the baseline can also be much less obvious. Use one of these less obvious baselines. Briefly state your example.

1 Change _____

2 Arbitrary baseline _____

3 Initial reaction _____

4 Full impact of change _____

5 Delayed reaction _____

6 Consequences to you and your organization _____

Here is another example of a baseline for change that was missed badly.

Harvey Kellerman, the chairman of the board for a metropolitan hospital, had for many years been successful in producing a steady stream of "giving" to supplement operating deficits or for spearheading capital expenditures involving building and equipment. Asked to assume the major responsibility for directing a new fund drive, Kellerman pointed out that the growing inflation rate and erosion of corporate profits were making funds development a much tougher undertaking. Kellerman felt he had done his turn and that this was hardly a period to start a new capital funds drive. "We've got to ride this thing out," he told the board. "Companies don't have the profits, and individual funds are tied up in depressed stocks. If we go after them now, we'll get people upset and turn them off for future approaches. It's not worth it." Shortly after his statement to the board, two other hospitals announced major fund drives. Both of these hospitals met their capital funds goals, which were set at all-time highs. Furthermore, these efforts tapped corporate, foundation, and individual sources that had in the past contributed generously to Kellerman's hospital. It became increasingly clear to Kellerman that despite his analysis of economic conditions he had failed to identify an important point from which to anticipate the effects of change. This missed baseline was the decision on the part of the other hospitals to launch fund drives. Taking full account of this decision as a change would have caused Kellerman to review his own position in light of the competition for funds.

Thinking Ahead

The real challenge is, of course, to pose the question HOW DOES CHANGE AFFECT ME? early enough to do something about it. But assessing the impact of change is not always easy. Even if you have a pretty good idea of what is going on in your immediate and surrounding environment, you can still fail to assess what is in store for you personally. The fact is that the consequences of many changes—probably most—can never be fully known. Nevertheless, raising the question is what matters. Doing so allows you to think beyond the here and now to confront yourself with possible options before change forecloses on them.

Asking yourself how change affects you is not always easy. There are times when it may seem preferable to let destiny take its course. This may be a valid way to deal with life, but then again it may simply be a way of covering a fear of coming to grips with the future. Wishful thinking is a variation on this cover: You ask yourself the question but accept only those conclusions that seem positive and rosy. There is also the other side of the same coin: accepting only those conclusions that are dark and dreary. Then you can rationalize, "How can anyone cope with such a rotten outlook? Better just to ride out the wave."

And, finally, you can honestly ask yourself the question of how change affects you and honestly arrive at the wrong conclusions anyway, without playing games. So stay flexible.

Two More to Think About

So far we have considered two basic questions:

> WHERE HAS CHANGE TAKEN PLACE?
> HOW DOES CHANGE AFFECT ME?

These two interrelated questions help get the real issues concerning change out in the open. The next two questions will help you manage change more effectively once you have it in perspective. They have a two-way cause-and-effect relationship:

> DO I HAVE THE ABILITIES TO CHANGE?
> DO I WANT TO CHANGE?

Feeling that you are able to change helps you answer whether you want to change—and vice versa. Wanting to change, you may find that indeed you have the abilities to change.

Abilities and Attitudes

The *abilities* needed for any change are (1) those directly related to the nature of the task involved in the change, and (2) those required to sustain the activity. For example, suppose an electronics technician is considering starting her own business. She needs to ask herself if she has (1) the basic technical and business knowledge to make the change possible. These are the abilities directly related to the initial change of going into business. She also needs to determine if she has (2) the capacity for working longer hours and living on a smaller initial income. These are the abilities required to sustain the change.

When it comes to the question DO I WANT TO CHANGE? the would-be owner needs to ask herself if she has positive and strong *attitudes* toward having her own business, such as willingness to take on financial risk, give up job security, be self-reliant, accept personal accountability, possible failure, family considerations, and general concern about tomorrow. Abilities and attitudes both count in explaining readiness for change.

Consider how abilities and attitudes play connecting roles in changes in your own life. There has no doubt been more than one instance where you found you had the abilities to make a particular change and were therefore motivated toward the change. It may have been a change in the focus of your education after you discovered you had a particular aptitude. Or it may have been job related. The following exercise will give you an opportunity to connect these notions of abilities and attitudes with events in your personal life.

How Abilities Fostered Attitude Toward Making a Change

Recall an incident where your skills or abilities encouraged you to make a change.

_____

_____

continued

How Abilities Fostered Attitude Toward Making a Change (continued)

_____
_____

How High Motivation Led to Developing Skills for Making a Change

Describe a situation where high motivation (attitude) to accomplish something encouraged you to acquire the necessary training for skills.

_____
_____
_____

In principle, as in the two examples you just cited, the questions related to ability to change and desire for change call for separate consideration. But *in reality*, the answer to either one is likely to influence the other. In appraising response to change, it helps to recognize just how the dice are loaded. We will look more closely at this aspect of managing change in the next chapter.

Action Checklist

1 Can you identify changes taking place both within and outside of your organization that affect you?   Yes ____ No ____

2 Are you able to follow changes underway and see when and/or how they will affect you, your work, or areas of responsibility?   Yes ____ No ____

3 Do you have a plan or some methods for dealing with current or emergent changes?   Yes ____ No ____

4 Are you developing baselines to assist in judging the relative magnitude and scope of change as well as its potential potency?   Yes ____ No ____

continued

Action Checklist (continued)

5   Does part of your coping strategy for change include periodic self-examination of your abilities and approaches for dealing with change?   Yes ____   No ____

6   Are you checking your sense of change with associates in some way?   Yes ____   No ____

Reacting to Change 3

Even when you say you want to change, deep down part of you just doesn't want to.

CHAPTER 1	CHAPTER 2	CHAPTER 3	CHAPTER 4
Situational Pressures for Change	Four Questions 1 Where has change taken place? 2 How does change affect me? 3 Do I have the abilities to change? 4 Do I want to change?	**Reacting to Change**	Organizational Change and Systems Thinking

CHAPTER 5	CHAPTERS 6, 7, 8	CHAPTERS 9, 10	CHAPTER 11
Goals for Change	Strategies for Change	Managing the Change Plan	New Sources and Directions for Change

CHAPTER 12, APPENDIXES

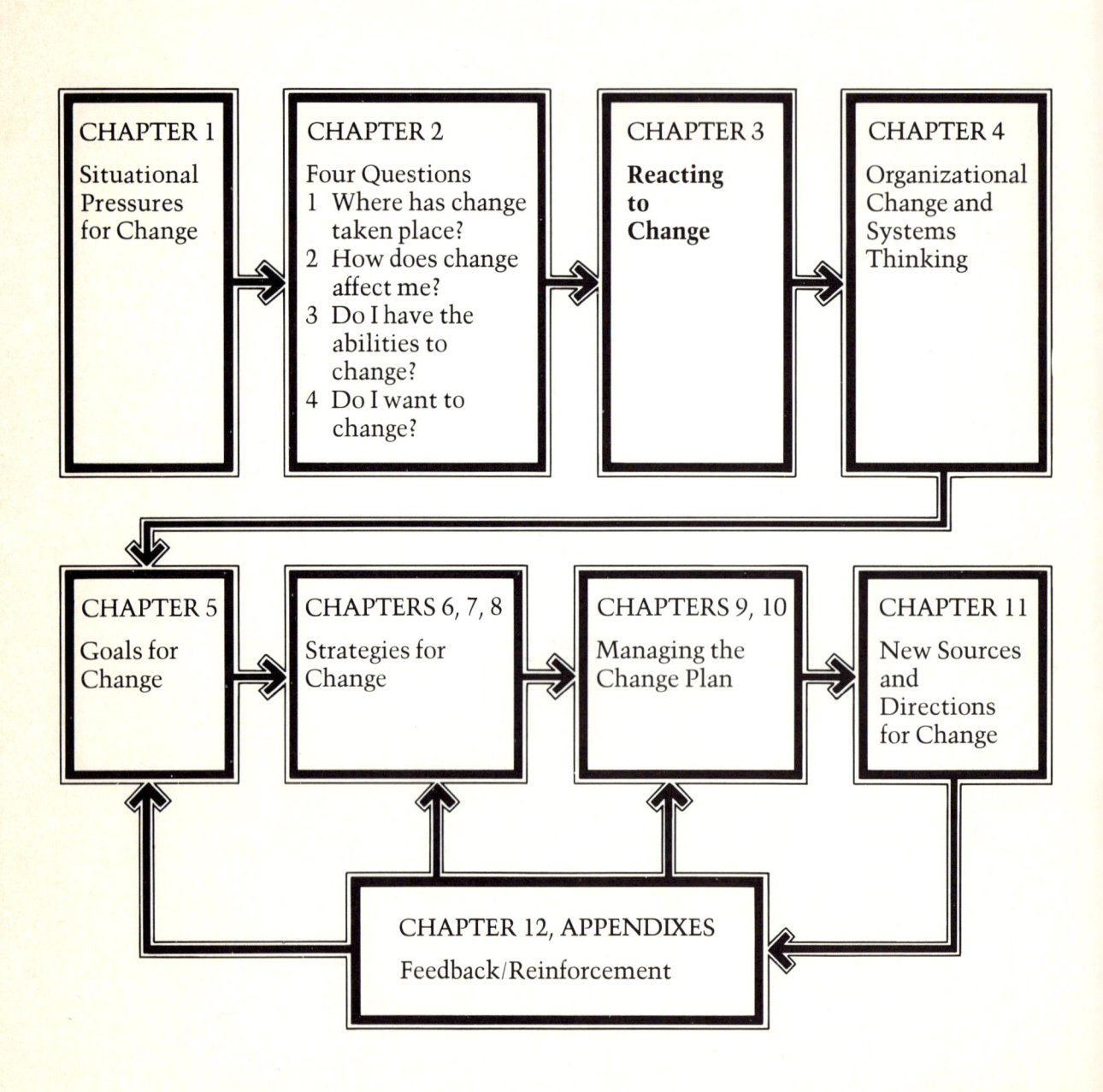

Feedback/Reinforcement

If change is ongoing everywhere, why is resistance to change such a common reaction? You know the answer, of course. It revolves around the last of our four basic questions: DO I WANT TO CHANGE? And the answer often is, No, I don't. Even when you say you want to change and realize you should—or must—deep down part of you just doesn't want to.

It's not often stated so bluntly. Usually some reason is given to the effect that the change being considered would be uneconomical or unwise. And that might be the case. Separating pronouncements of fact from personal concern is not easy. Clearly, they are linked. We invariably favor our view of things or a situation by inner feelings and concerns. It is important to be sensitive to this link, for even when the need for change is clear, there is often deep-seated personal resistance. People don't like change.

It's more than just a simple expression of preference. It's more than human perversity or cowardice. It's a feeling for survival. Change is a threat to survival. Change means unpredictability. And unpredictability means danger.

The Need for Predictability

Coping with daily events and planning for the future are dependent on correctly anticipating what is going to happen—predictability. When you answer the telephone, you expect to hear a voice on the other end. When you turn on the television, you expect to see a picture appear on the screen. If one day the telephone delivered an electric shock or the television erupted in flames, you would approach both devices more gingerly the next time around. Your sense of predictability in them would have been shaken.

If you put a percentage of your regular income in a savings account each month, you expect the principal to grow and accrue interest. If you work diligently at your job, you expect eventual advancement and an increase in pay. If one day the bank were to close its doors or you were summarily fired, you would be equally shocked by the abrupt change. Your long and carefully, sometimes painfully, acquired knowledge of cause-and-effect connections would be jolted. Your predictability gyroscope would be knocked for a loop. No less shocking in this regard are the investment and savings plans that turn out to have hardly matched the inflation rate, let alone to have accrued sufficient funds for special usage or retirement.

Putting Up Resistance

Resistance to change is in part a result of such unsettling experiences. As long as things are going along in a predictable way, you know how to cope. You are on safe ground. But when something unexpected happens, you have to stop to think about the next step. The old way won't work anymore. You are back to square one. Clearly, there is a need for monitoring the environment for new change focus, as in the case of investment funds and inflation. The "unexpected" resulted from not following the trends and considering alternate investment possibilities (for example, bonds or land).

But you resist change, even if change is inevitable. Putting up resistance is a way of gaining some time to think (or at least an illusion of gaining time) about what to do next, how to cope with the new situation. Two elements are involved. The first is attempting to predict the direction the change will take or what will eventually happen. The second is coming up with an adequate set of responses (DO I HAVE THE ABILITIES TO CHANGE?).

The sales manager whose position is about to be affected under a new organizational structure may do his best to convince management that the new scheme is flawed, both as part of his resistance and as an attempt to test out how the scheme may eventually affect him. At the same time, he will be privately considering how to use his experience to qualify for a new position either with the same organization or with a new one. He is trying to stabilize his predictability gyroscope. And all the while, of course, he is trying to resolve the conflicting sides of the question DO I WANT TO CHANGE?

A Many-Sided Question

The following scenario illustrates some of the many sides of DO I WANT TO CHANGE? The change in question is a pervasive one—the expanding career opportunities for women.

Mary Wolfe was employed as production assistant for a small advertising agency. The work was dull, but her associates were pleasant and the job was only a short commute from her home. When the agency was bought out by a larger firm, changes began to be apparent to Wolfe. Her work load increased markedly. She was called on to make production decisions she had never had to make before. The easy sociability of former times seemed to evaporate under increased pressure and stress. She could no longer leave her job at the office. At home in the evenings, more and more she found herself worrying about whether she had made the right decision that day and fretting over mistakes she knew she had made.

When the production manager announced that he was being transferred, Mary felt that this was the last straw. She was seriously considering quitting. But before she could, her department head did the "unpredictable." He offered her the job of production manager. It meant an increase in pay and much greater say-so concerning procedures and scheduling. She asked for some time to consider. She didn't know if she could handle the new position. And she wasn't sure she really wanted it.

Finishing the Scenario

Change does not take place in a vacuum. Mary Wolfe probably has the abilities she needs to succeed as production manager. That seems evident from her conscientious performance on the job before the position was offered to her. It was no doubt clear to management that she was capable of increased responsibility and was probably holding herself back.

There are a number of ways to finish the scenario of Mary Wolfe. We can have her take the new position and succeed. We can have her take the new position and fail. Or we can have her refuse the new position and stay where she is. These three options and others are available to each of us in various change situations. Whichever one is chosen, some degree of change will take place. For a moment, let's look more closely at the decisions facing Mary Wolfe.

Mary Wolfe's Decision Situation

Issue: Shall I take the job of production manager? Alternatives that I have identified thus far:

1. Accept job.
2. Turn down the job but stay on with the firm.
3. Turn down the job but try to arrange a transfer to a less stressful situation.
4. Turn down the job but start looking for other possibilities.
5. Simply quit and develop my career elsewhere.

Put yourself in Wolfe's position and consider the five alternatives outlined above. For each alternative, list both pros and cons.

Alternatives	Pros	Cons
1 Accept	_____	_____
	_____	_____
	_____	_____
	_____	_____
2 Turn down, stay	_____	_____
	_____	_____
	_____	_____
	_____	_____

continued

Mary Wolfe's Decision Situation (continued)

Alternatives	Pros	Cons
3 Turn down, transfer		
4 Turn down, job search		
5 Quit		

Reasons Behind Reactions

You probably found it easier to list the pros for some of the possibilities and found it easier to list the cons for others. Some of the pros or cons no doubt seemed more likely or came more rapidly to mind. But the odds are that in all five cases there were certain things in common. In all five you probably listed the same or very similar feelings behind Wolfe's resistance to change (and your own).

The decision facing her involves many complex factors. Uncertainty and unpredictability are two obvious ones. She is unsure of her abilities to qualify for the higher level job. She is not even sure that she wants to move in this direction. She is uncertain as to what to expect in assuming the manager's job.

Mary Wolfe can justifiably ask, "DO I WANT TO CHANGE?" She needs more information. She needs to know more about herself and what she wants to do. She needs to know more about what the manager's job entails and how this fits in with her capabilites and with her current and future needs. Her personal reaction to change is a response to uncertainty and to the unknown. Such a response can be a valuable signal to the individual of the need to gain information and perspective regarding the change situation. A vital way of gaining perspective is by examining personal feelings about resistance to change. Securing more data and checking your sense of the situation with others are two practical ways of dealing with this change issue.

Personal Feelings and Response

Fear, lack of confidence, and uncertainty are three different ways of describing similar feelings. Whatever name this queasy feeling is given, it is the most common cause of resistance to change, the most common feeling that discourages a person from risking the unknown.

It may be fear of being caught without the answers—know-how, skills, or confidence in your ability to master a situation. It may be a specific fear, such as loss of your job, or a more diffuse fear, such as the thought of not being able to find any suitable employment. Some people even fear success, for they cannot imagine (predict!) what life would be like under such circumstances.

Lack of confidence in your ability to predict what is to come, even in a general way, causes resistance to change. It may be the result of past unsettling experiences that unbalanced your predictability gyroscope. This is not to say that anybody has a special crystal ball that gives him a more certain view of the future than yours. But the art of planning and prediction has improved with better analysis and computer-based methods. Prediction power has also been bolstered by *how* we look at things, the system view (discussed later), and *where* we look for clues. In short, better methods of improving predictability have emerged. But knowledge of these methods is only part of strengthening one's confidence in anticipating change. Mental state and outlook is still the ultimate determinant of confidence in prediction abilities.

Another concern that causes resistance to change is personal status. With change, your status may be at stake through exposure and judgment by other people. It is understandable that many individuals prefer to remain untested by change, both with regard to themselves and others.

There is also a strong need for continuity in our lives. Being reasonably sure about what will take place tomorrow and the day after enables you to develop a *personal time horizon* and frees you to go about your business. Uncertainty clouds that horizon. At very least, it is distracting. At worst, it may paralyze thought and action.

The Inconvenience Factor

Change may also mean sheer inconvenience or breaking a comfortable lifestyle. Patterns of life, including physical habits and surroundings, frame of mind, personal relationships, and work achievements do not come into being either quickly or easily. Furthermore, each habit, relationship, and achievement is supported by a host of peripheral activities. You may have finally located the perfect restaurant, found true friends, gotten elected to the city council, or become vice-president of the company. Once established in a way of life and work, you may be too comfortable or too weary to accept, let alone welcome, modifications of present arrangements. When ambitions have been even partially realized, it is understandable to wish to coast awhile and enjoy the fruits of the effort—and to respond negatively to DO I WANT TO CHANGE?

Another facet of the inconvenience factor has to do with separating organizational responsibilities and necessities from personal preferences or lifestyle: carrying out job responsibilities in an efficient or imaginative way may be "interfering" with or disrupting lifestyle patterns. For example, field sales problems might indicate spending more time with out-of-town sales people, and for a rather indefinite period. Your tennis game, community affairs, or other activities would be disrupted. Understandably, you would be reluctant to undertake this type of major change in business-related activities. In the short run, you might be willing to put up with some inconvenience. If the change indicates a longer-run personal adjustment, you would have to view the alternatives clearly and honestly in terms of organizational necessities and personal preference. Thus, the notion of DO I WANT TO CHANGE? argues for sensitivity to these types of issues: keeping business and personal matters as sharply defined as possible—and then making decisions to resolve these issues before even more complex ones arise.

Idealizing the Present, and the Seven Deadly Sins

Under threat of change, there is often a tendency to idealize the present. Things may suddenly seem better, their undersirable qualities conveniently slipping away. This is a familiar enough phenomenon to anyone who has ever parted with a lover, embarked on a new job, or moved to a different part of the country.

Beyond sentimentality, this idealization represents a longing for the comfort and security of a prior state of life, association, or organization. Lover, job, or home—all seem rather wondrous and irreplaceable in contrast to the uncertainty, unfamiliarity, and general bother of getting used to new objects and relationships and developing new habits. As the pressure mounts to give up what you have, for whatever reason, the status quo may appear rosier and rosier.

Deeper, less "acceptable" feelings contribute to this idealization of the present, such as dependency, laziness, insecurity, lust, greed, pride, and egomania. These are left unsaid and sometimes even unthought, but they act nonetheless as powerful incentives for avoiding change. Staying with the present setup is a way of protecting vested interests of personal significance, albeit sometimes obscure ones.

Does Change Equal Progress?

Finally, a change may be resisted on its own terms. The change may go against your better judgment. Such judgment may be grounded in past experience or special knowledge of the matter at hand, an alternate assessment of costs or benefits, and may be quite independent of other factors (your hidden agenda), such as those just discussed. The following is an example:

Leah Keiller was a successful clothing buyer who had been with Laporte's, a large department store, for some years. When the store was remodeled in an attempt to appeal to younger, more affluent customers, Keiller was reluctant to go along with management's recommendation that she create a new image for her department. She argued that her customers were established and conservative and knew what they wanted. She pointed out that there were other outlets for the kind of items (and image) management wanted but that her clientele did not patronize them. Nonetheless, Keiller agreed to go along with the change and threw herself into it wholeheartedly. In spite of her best efforts, sales in her unit declined. As time went by, Keiller was forced to reintroduce a few of the styles her customers continued to ask for. Management tacitly went along with it.

Resisting a change on its own terms usually does not receive the acknowledgment it deserves. Usually there is suspicion that change is being resisted for some ulterior motive. Such resistance is seen as simple obstructionism and is not looked upon favorably by those desiring the change. But not all change equals progress, nor is all conservatism reactionary. Opponents of change may have sound reasons for their views, a possibility that should be accepted by all who are concerned with understanding reactions to change. What is important for everyone involved is that they understand the factors for encouraging or resisting change and to agree on criteria for evaluating change.

Chapter 3

The Need to Change

Our general experience is that the answer to DO I WANT TO CHANGE? is more often than not negative. Yet there is within many people a deep-seated positive sense about change. If this seems paradoxical, the difficulty may rest with the idea that the desire for change may sometimes seem irrational when change does not seem for the better. But the desire is there anyway. This deep-rooted feeling is often a precondition for personal growth. The development of both children and adults is retarded in a static environment, and a drive to seek novelty may be as basic as the drives that assure life itself.

We get restless when we have gone too long without a change. Change may allow us to test our personal potential—possible strengths, convictions, dormant talents—in short, to try out aspects of the self that do not find expression in current patterns of our organizational or personal lives. A new lease on life may result, or at least an extension of the rental agreement.

To examine how this need for change works, think of a situation where you caused change to happen even though the prevailing circumstances were outwardly agreeable. It may have been a personal relationship, a job-related situation, or a change in lifestyle. It may have been getting married or getting divorced, getting fired or getting hired. Because the basic human need for change is so deeply rooted, you may not have even been fully aware of how you set up the change situation.

What was the change situation?
_____
_____

First, let's deal with the conditions before change took place. Some people may have seen the situation as it was as perfectly agreeable. Others may have seen the proposed change as one actually worsening the situation. Enter these two ideas below.

1 Situation fine the way it was

_____
_____

Change seen as worsening the situation

_____
_____

Second, let's recognize that a change situation can have many unfulfilling aspects although the final result is positive. Enter these two ideas below.

2 Aspects of situation that were unfulfilling

_____
_____

The final positive result

_____
_____

Your reexamination of the event from different viewpoints probably brought out circumstances surrounding the change. It's likely that an early reading of the considerations would probably have been negative. The fact that this kind of situation is so common indicates that we should start to develop general approaches to change that are systematic and minimize the occurrence of premature responses that may signal "go" or "stop."

The Ambivalence Factor

Change is to a large extent whatever you personally feel counts. As the last exercise may have demonstrated, it is also to a large extent just what it seems to you to be—positive, negative, or both. It is understandable, then, that change is often approached in an ambivalent fashion. Even "welcome" change usually arouses anxiety, and at times "decisions" are made for us that help resolve things long left unsettled. For example, when the shock wears off, the person fired without warning may feel more liberated than at loose ends. A decision for change has been made for him that he knew should have been made long ago but just couldn't bring himself to make.

As mentioned, rejection or acceptance of change may have little to do with the merits or drawbacks of the proposed change itself. Further, in attempting to understand attitudes and feelings toward change-related problems, keep in mind that resistance and acceptance are two sides of the same coin; both sets of feelings are present in *all* reactions to change. To perceive only one side of the coin is to miss the reality of the whole coin.

Individual Similarities and Differences

Attitudes toward change are the result of personal characteristics and individual experiences. Thus, people differ in the extent to which they are likely to accept, reject, or impose change. We may never have sufficient knowledge to "explain" any one person but to some degree propensities can be predicted.

Groupthink and Methink

Of course, as none of us grows up in isolation, we are indeed all members of groups. And it is true that affiliation with these groups contributes to the shaping of values and feelings about change. Family, religious, ethnic, and organizational affiliations, sex, and other group memberships all are shaping forces.

A person's age is another determiner of reactions to change. Older people, taken as a group, have broader and longer personal histories against which to weigh change. The security that tends to accrue with age—in both material and social investments—is also a factor. However, the stereotype of the conservative older person versus the change-happy youngster, like other group stereotypes, is a gross oversimplification.

While older people *as a group* are more conservative, you cannot predict how an *individual member of that group* is going to react to change. The security, responsibilities, or health problems that come with age may tend to make a person conservative. But age may also make some changes possible for that person, and increasing numbers of multiple careers reflect this ability and freedom to act. In the end, *methink* frequently overrides groupthink. It pays for anyone managing change to recognize the hold of both sets of factors.

Groupthink and Methink Factors in Change

To hammer the idea of methink home, consider five groups of which you are a member. These may be broad groups such as male/female or ethnic affiliation or more specific groups such as professions, community organizations, or sports fans, or vegetarians. Tell how the group as a whole would be characterized about a particular issue or event. Then describe some way in which you differ from the group opinion.

	Group	Issue or event	Groupthink	Methink
1	_____	_____	_____	_____
2	_____	_____	_____	_____
3	_____	_____	_____	_____
4	_____	_____	_____	_____
5	_____	_____	_____	_____
6	_____	_____	_____	_____

Chapter 3

The Final Analysis

There is always uncertainty about what an individual might do or not do. No one is completely predictable, either as a member of a group or as an individual. Each of us, like life itself, is complex. Recognizing the forces which contribute to this complexity is the starting point to understanding any individual's reaction to change—your own or someone else's.

Action Checklist

1 Can you trace the effects of change on events or activities important to you? Yes ____ No ____

2 Have you enlarged your understanding about how changes in personnel, in terms of race and sex, are affecting your work activity and those around you? Yes ____ No ____

3 Can you identify groupthink and methink elements of change matters with which you are concerned? Yes ____ No ____

4 Can you identify the factors contributing to fears, lack of confidence, or uncertainties faced by you or those you work with? Yes ____ No ____

5 Can you identify those around you who appear to welcome or resist change and understand why this is so? Yes ____ No ____

6 Are you developing approaches to a person who resists change because of habit or idealization of the present? Yes ____ No ____

7 Where legitimate reasons appear to exist for resisting change, can you set up an accounting for or against? Yes ____ No ____

Sorting Things Out 4

Awareness is a powerful tool in dealing with change.

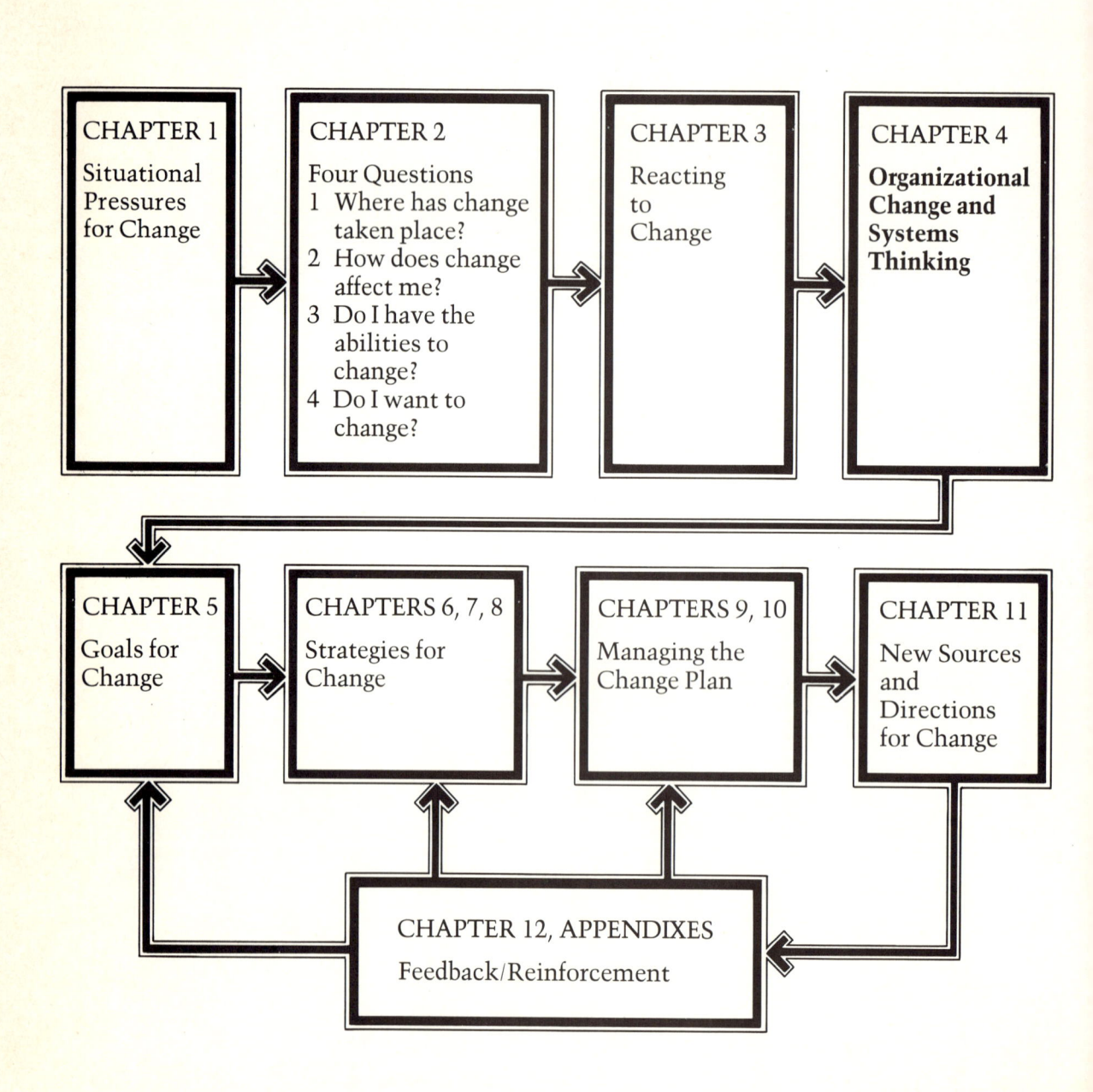

CHAPTER 1	CHAPTER 2	CHAPTER 3	CHAPTER 4
Situational Pressures for Change	Four Questions 1. Where has change taken place? 2. How does change affect me? 3. Do I have the abilities to change? 4. Do I want to change?	Reacting to Change	**Organizational Change and Systems Thinking**

CHAPTER 5	CHAPTERS 6, 7, 8	CHAPTERS 9, 10	CHAPTER 11
Goals for Change	Strategies for Change	Managing the Change Plan	New Sources and Directions for Change

CHAPTER 12, APPENDIXES

Feedback/Reinforcement

The aim so far has been to increase your awareness of change, and to drive home the point that you *define* as well as react to change. Such awareness is a powerful tool in dealing with change.

Against this backdrop, we now turn specifically to change that must be responded to, planned for, or carried out in organizational life. The spotlight is on the manager rather than the organization. We don't feel obliged to sell you on your organization or to teach you how to live with it happily ever after, but what follows should improve your ability to steer within it.

In this chapter, you will become sharper at sensing organizational change (WHERE HAS CHANGE TAKEN PLACE?), understanding what it means for you (HOW DOES CHANGE AFFECT ME?), and recognizing clearly the issues this raises.

Systems thinking is introduced as a useful tool for sizing things up. This *way of thinking* about processes, problems, and changes makes it possible to connect internal organizational developments and needs to the broader arena—the external environment. It also relates internal events to each other and to the organization as a whole. Systems thinking can be applied to all levels of organization. In this chapter, you will be asked to try it out on a problem of your own.

Two (Organizational) Questions

First, let's consider the questions raised in Chapter 1 in the light of organizational change:

WHERE HAS (ORGANIZATIONAL) CHANGE TAKEN PLACE?

The answer may strike you as self-evident: The changes are obvious. But let's probe beyond the obvious. Even though the processes of change are all around us in organizational life, many go unnoticed as instances of change. For example, training is one of the most widely undertaken activities in organizations. Training involves change—developing new skills and modifying old ones—but it is not always recognized as such. Other common change-related activities—procedural changes, promotion to new assignments, unionization of an employer—interlace the work world. You can name many more. Once you see these activities as *changes taking place,* rather than "business as usual," reexamine the second question:

HOW DOES (ORGANIZATIONAL) CHANGE AFFECT ME?

Of course, you are—or will be—affected by changes taking place. Your organization may be big enough or worried enough to hire a "Change Agent," a specialist who diagnoses and makes recommendations for change. Whether or not this is the case, each member of an organization must (and does) function as a change agent, without benefit of the capital letters. You may have to implement the recommendations or instructions of others to bring about change. Or you may be required to take the initiative in forecasting and planning for needed change. In either event, organizational change is touching you. When you recognize this, you will also realize that *you have strategies for dealing with change.* These may be largely intuitive, but they are nonetheless real. You can make these strategies work more effectively for you by examining your operating assumptions. What are your hunches and convictions based on? How do they relate to other parts of your organization? How complete is your information? What outcomes can you expect?

Limitations of Objectivity

Like the story about the three blind men describing the elephant, we all tend to form conclusions based on partial knowledge. But even with perfect vision, no two people view either elephants or organizations from the same place. Consider one department of a bank, an organization with which everyone is familiar.

It gradually became apparent that a rash of time-consuming errors in the operations department was associated with lack of cooperation among the newer tellers. Henry Collins, manager of the department, called a meeting to discuss the problem with some key people. Collins thought that work procedures needed to be changed to reduce the need for certain teller decisions. Elizabeth Bergson, who supervised the tellers, blamed things on her own work overload and consequent inability to provide adequate supervision. Margaret Brown, a senior employee and assistant to the manager, felt the real cause was intense competition for a single upcoming opportunity for promotion. Irene McCoy, the personnel director, observed that the situation was typical of the new generation of workers who failed to identify with their organizations or take their jobs very seriously. When questioned, the tellers themselves presented an equal variety of explanations; some couldn't understand what all the fuss was about since "everybody makes mistakes."

The reactions at the bank help illustrate three important points regarding all organizations:

1 There are many ways to view events.

2 No particular view necessarily qualifies as *the* reality.

3 In order to understand, deal with, or change a situation, it is necessary to take account of many realities.

This is where systems thinking comes in. Fuller consideration of relevant factors helps to remove the blinders that limit and distort vision. In turn, this helps to determine essential needs and to establish priorities.

Systems and Systems Thinking

Systems thinking means viewing the organization in terms of its larger environment and treating the organization both as a whole and as a set of intricately related parts. To some extent, we all think along these lines. But we generally fail to carry the analysis of the system very far.

Take the bank as an example of a system. A bank is a system in that it is an organization operating over an extended period, composed of interdependent parts, and faced with the need to adjust to the outside world.

An organization *never reaches a stable level of existence*, no matter how well things are operating. The organization always exists in a larger environment such as neighborhood, region, or country and must adapt to social, economic, and political changes occurring at each level. Banking interest rates and lending policies obviously reflect such changes, but system adaptation may also result, for example, in terms of new organizational functions or products. Banks, to be sure, are primarily in the business of receiving and lending money, but competition and changing public needs have resulted in expansion of their services, along with changed means for ensuring their share of the market (such as drive-in facilities and gifts for depositors). Further adaptation is required because of changing internal conditions—new employees are coming in, and others quitting or retiring. In addition, the traditional division of labor has been disrupted by computerization. The point at which decisions are made, the distribution of personnel between departments, and the relative number and types of managers and support personnel have changed. These in turn have called for both new procedures and new skills.

Truths About All Organizations

The points made about the bank as a system apply to all organizations. All organizations must respond and adapt to ever-changing external and internal conditions. All organizations have an internal division of work tasks, which creates differing reactions to the needs or problems facing the overall system. This, in turn, creates unavoidable tensions among the parts. All organizations have interaction between external and internal circumstances, which may eventually bring about change in organizational goals, products, or services.

An additional point related to the organization of work is worth stressing. Not everyone in an organization is consciously or equally occupied with general organizational goals. Divisions, departments, or smaller work units are often preoccupied with the immediacy of "their" own problems. Thus, the things that really get to us—whether as vice presidents or bank tellers—are more related to the way in which organizational requirements affect *immediate* responsibilities as well as personal values and needs.

To understand any system, then, it is necessary to take account of the range of influences that operate *within* and *beyond* system boundaries to determine the needs of the system as a whole and the differences among its parts. Most important, it is the *reciprocal* and *multidirectional* nature of these effects that must be understood. Actions that originate at any level or in any part of a system have repercussions elsewhere within it. This in turn means new consequences for the system. For example, the enforcement of equal opportunity legislation has forced a number of organizations to change their personnel practices. These effects have been felt throughout the organization but in widely different forms and degrees. And in some cases these have come into conflict with collective bargaining or certain business practices. In turn, this has led to re-examination of the original planned-for changes with various types of mutual accommodation resulting.

Determining *how it all hangs together* is the essence of systems thinking. Such an approach is less likely to define *the* problem or locate the blame in any *one* part. Neither will it give you final answers—since no one has all the information and systems keep on changing. You should, however, arrive at a better description of the "elephants" in your organizational life, and from there it is easier to decide what to do.

The Scope of Systems Analysis

A relatively large and well-developed body of procedures, models, and methods has emerged over the past twenty years to strengthen systems approaches. Many of these are well known to organization members. Since this is not a book on systems management per se, this subject matter goes beyond the development of a systems perspective, which is the primary concern in the present discussion. It is important, however, to recognize the scope of work that has evolved in this area. For example:

- **Analytical methods**

    - various programming techniques (e.g., "linear") that take into account jointly the various resources of an organization.

    - mathematical models such as "Marken" that assist in analyzing complex flows among interrelated functions.

- **Computer-related systems and procedures**

    - explicit treatment of the interdependencies and relationships among people and events.

- **Planning and control models and charting techniques**

    - PERT, CPM, and a large group of network-charting techniques and models that tie together activities, time, and even costs.

    - Gantt-type charts—an older, yet widely used, approach for charting interrelated activities over time.

- **Organizational behavioral approaches**

  - Organization Development (discussed in Chapter 8), which deals with the working relationships within *and* between organizational units.

This listing suggests how far systems thinking has progressed. It also suggests the wealth of approaches available to organization members.

Trying a Systems Approach

Systems thinking is not confined to problem solving. For our purposes, however, let's apply it to an organizational problem from your own experience. Think of a problem related to change and of special importance to you. To assist you, a parallel point will be drawn from the bank example for each step of the analysis.

1 What is the problem in your organization as *you* see it?

At the bank each member of the operations department saw things in his or her own way. State your version of your organization problem in two or three sentences. This is easier said than done, but brevity will help you to clarify your opinions by making you get to the heart of the matter.

Definition of an organizational problem _____

_____

_____

_____

_____

_____

continued

2 Does the source of your problem appear to lie *within* the organization or *outside* the organization (and system)?

Problems that originate outside the system are not as controllable as those that have internal origins.

In emphasizing work procedures, Henry Collins, the department manager, located the source within the system—a source he had considerable control over. For Irene McCoy, the personnel director, the problem was rooted in the general social climate—*outside* the department and the bank as well. She therefore saw the problem as one she could do little about.

Problem
source—
within or
outside the
organization?
_____
_____
_____
_____

3 Is the source of your organization problem a *recurring* or a *one-time* event?

Problems are either one-time events or recurring events. Recurring problems are more difficult to minimize or ignore. Seeing problems in recurring terms also promotes establishing a pattern for dealing with similar events in the future.

Henry Collins felt the situation at the bank was chronic, demanding the development of a specific approach to deal with it. His assistant, Margaret Brown, in stressing the one-time promotion opportunity, underestimated the whole matter, at least as a chronic problem.

Problem
source—
recurring or
one-time event?
_____
_____
_____
_____

4 *Who* is affected by your organization problem?

Is the problem essentially yours alone or does it affect others? Does it touch an entire group, department, or the whole organization?

Everyone in a system is affected by what takes place in any one part, but some individuals feel the effects more fully. And some are more aware of the magnitude of the problem than others.

Some of the tellers felt there was no problem. Henry saw the problem as involving himself, the entire staff of tellers, and their supervisor.

continued

Who is
affected
within the
organization? _____
                _____
                _____
                _____
                _____

5 *What* is affected by your organization problem?

In looking at what is affected by organizational change, there are three levels to consider: the organization as a whole, subunits, and individuals. An organizational effect might be loss of business or profits; a given department might experience rapid turnover or low morale; an individual might be affected in terms of income, health, or self-respect. Again, effects are never independent of each other, but you should make an attempt to identify each to ensure full consideration of the problem.

Taking the operations department as a whole, one effect was strained relations among members. Elizabeth Bergson, the supervisor, felt that her efficiency record was at stake. Time and energy, which should have been applied to other duties, were important costs to Henry Collins, the department manager. A primary effect for the tellers was longer work hours to put things in order.

What is
affected
within the
organization? _____
                _____
                _____
                _____
                _____

6 What steps can you take about the effects you identified in point 5?

How would these steps be constructive? Which aspects require immediate attention? Identify these first. Then list those that will require longer-run attention.

Once he understood how the problem affected his organization, the bank manager took steps to solve it. He assigned priority to working out more effective work routines. He relieved Elizabeth Bergson of extraneous duties so she could devote full attention to this. He saw other dimensions of the problem—such as limited chances for promotion—as requiring more time and thought.

continued

Possibilities and priorities for taking action	_____

To sum up, a systems thinking approach to organizational problems or issues involving changes consists of these steps:
1   problem definition
2   determination of problem sources, inside/outside the system
3   determination of problem as a recurring or one-time event
4   specification of who is affected
5   specification of what is affected
6   determination of strategies possible and advisable for action and corresponding priorities

The key to a systems approach is seeing the *interrelationships* that affect the definition and resolution of a problem. Each step helps point to important connections between external environment, work performance, formal and informal authority, and personal needs and qualities. At the bank, for example, the personnel director's awareness of trends beyond the system (the bank) influenced her advice regarding the tellers. The assistant to the department manager knew much about the problem as a result of informal communication with the tellers; transmitted to the department manager, this information influenced the formal approach to improving teller efficiency and later affected other parts of the system—namely, revision of promotion policies.

Once More, with Feeling

Having now taken a systems view of the problem you were asked to propose, you should have a better conception of what is involved—and what you are up against. Always keep in mind that there are many realities. This is extremely important. You have firmed up your *own* outlook. Now go back through the steps summarized above, this time responding as you think certain other key members of your organization might. You already have some notion about how others feel—more often than not *this is part of the problem*. Keeping this in mind, write down what you believe their responses would be.

Comparing these responses with your own, *what can you learn?* Do any alternatives emerge? In examining the many realities, you will be looking at the system as a set of intricately related parts. Then bring the parts together as facets of the whole. Jot down your thoughts on how it all hangs together.

Fresh perspectives on the organizational problem
_____
_____
_____
_____
_____

Broadening Your Horizons

It is very easy, and only human, to become bogged down in one version of the "truth" (probably a fuzzy one at that). The type of analysis you have just done may seem elementary, but thoughtfully applied it will lead to a sharper view of your change situation or problem—and of your problem in relationship to your organization as a whole.

If this procedure only confirms your original convictions, well and good, for you know you stand on comparatively solid ground. But very likely you now see some things in a different way. That difference may be important. Broadening your horizons through systems thinking, however, may also serve to increase frustrations—especially if you have to give up some pet beliefs and can't find promising new solutions. But even wheel spinning can be constructive if it causes you to ask DO I HAVE THE ABILITIES TO CHANGE? and DO I WANT TO CHANGE? The answers can lead to new statements of the problem—the equivalent of pumping new blood into the system.

Stopping Problems Before They Start

So far the emphasis has been on systems thinking as a way of grasping an interrelated whole, and thus increasing the possibilities for dealing with organizational problems related to change. But, as pointed out, systems thinking is by no means restricted to problem areas. Systems thinking can help you avoid new problems. Using it, you can anticipate the differing effects external changes may have on each part of an organization. By acting on these insights you can stop problems before they start. But this requires *sensitivity*.

The following example illustrates the need for sensitivity to the connection between environment and organization. It also reveals that when systems thinking is not sufficiently used to guide planning, many organizations are left unprepared to deal with change.

The passage of equal employment legislation some years ago signalled important changes for all types of organizations. Women, blacks, latins, and the economically disadvantaged, were, in theory at least, to receive employment opportunities on a par with the "white majority." Affirmative action programs were the logical outgrowth of this legislation, and organizations were to design and implement compliance programs.

Some organizations moved forward with little urging. For others, it was "business as usual." Finally, the increasing scope of enforcement action, community pressure, and publicity resulted in growing numbers of organizations adopting positive hiring programs.

Not even well-intentioned firms, however, fully anticipated the internal organizational preparation necessary to make programs successful. High turnover, conflict, low productivity, and considerable absenteeism plagued early programs. Just as many organizations missed the external impact of the legislation, many also missed the internal impact of these changes on supervisors, policies, and supportive activities needed for success. Policies had to be developed regarding training programs, promotion opportunities, and budgets. Supervisors had to be instructed and actively enlisted in these program efforts.

Systems thinking would have determined at an early point the likely relevance of equal opportunity legislation for the organization. It would have hastened recognizing the legislation as a permanent outside stimulus to organizational change and planning accordingly, rather than denying or ignoring the full implications. Secondly, systems thinking would have sought to establish not only the initial effects of these changes but also the second-round effects (such as the need for educating personnel to work cooperatively with new employees) as change penetrated the organization more widely and deeply.

What's Next?

We end this chapter with the same two questions with which we began:

> WHERE HAS CHANGE TAKEN PLACE?
> HOW DOES CHANGE AFFECT ME?

Ponder the first, however, in terms of events *beyond* rather than *within* your organization. Where might you be missing the boat? Consider the example involving equal employment legislation. What is the *next* wave of change going to be for your organization?

Existing environmental and safety legislation, rising consumer consciousness in new areas of concern, significant legal decisions, and political tensions throughout the world all point to present or future imperatives for change.

Give some thought to what this means for you and your organization, especially over an extended period of time. Don't worry if you don't have any ready answers. The answers just now are less important than your ability to keep on raising the questions.

In Brief

Once you realize that even ongoing organizational activities involve change, you are in a better position to anticipate and recognize the effects of this change—and to question your own, often unconscious, approaches to change.

Systems thinking is a means for increasing both awareness and objectivity. It directs attention to all aspects of a situation and to the interrelationships of these aspects. The resulting increase in your information yields better possibilities for dealing with change.

Systems thinking is valuable for more than problem solving. It stresses the *anticipation* of consequences among interrelated parts. Thus, it facilitates long-range planning for organizational response to change originating both within and outside the organization.

It follows that new goals result from systems thinking, and prevailing goals are called into question. The connections between goals and the change they actually promote are discussed in the next chapter.

Action Checklist

1 Can you identify some of your main assumptions (often unspoken) in your management techniques, leadership style, or simply relationships with others?   Yes____   No____

2 Have you been able to establish the completeness or adequacy of the information related to your assumptions?   Yes____   No____

3 Can you identify the dominant forces for change in your organization's external environment and how these are shaping policy and programs?   Yes____   No____

4 For a major change problem or issue with which you are now dealing, can you identify its source(s) and thereby your ability to influence the matter?   Yes____   No____

5 From a systems viewpoint, can you identify the interrelated people, organization units, and events tied to the change you are considering?   Yes____   No____

6 Are you able to develop a plan for action that includes both near-term and longer-run change priorities?   Yes____   No____

Goals for Change 5

A concrete goal is not necessarily a realistic one.

CHAPTER 1	CHAPTER 2	CHAPTER 3	CHAPTER 4
Situational Pressures for Change	Four Questions 1 Where has change taken place? 2 How does change affect me? 3 Do I have the abilities to change? 4 Do I want to change?	Reacting to Change	Organizational Change and Systems Thinking

CHAPTER 5	CHAPTERS 6, 7, 8	CHAPTERS 9, 10	CHAPTER 11
Goals for Change	Strategies for Change	Managing the Change Plan	New Sources and Directions for Change

CHAPTER 12, APPENDIXES

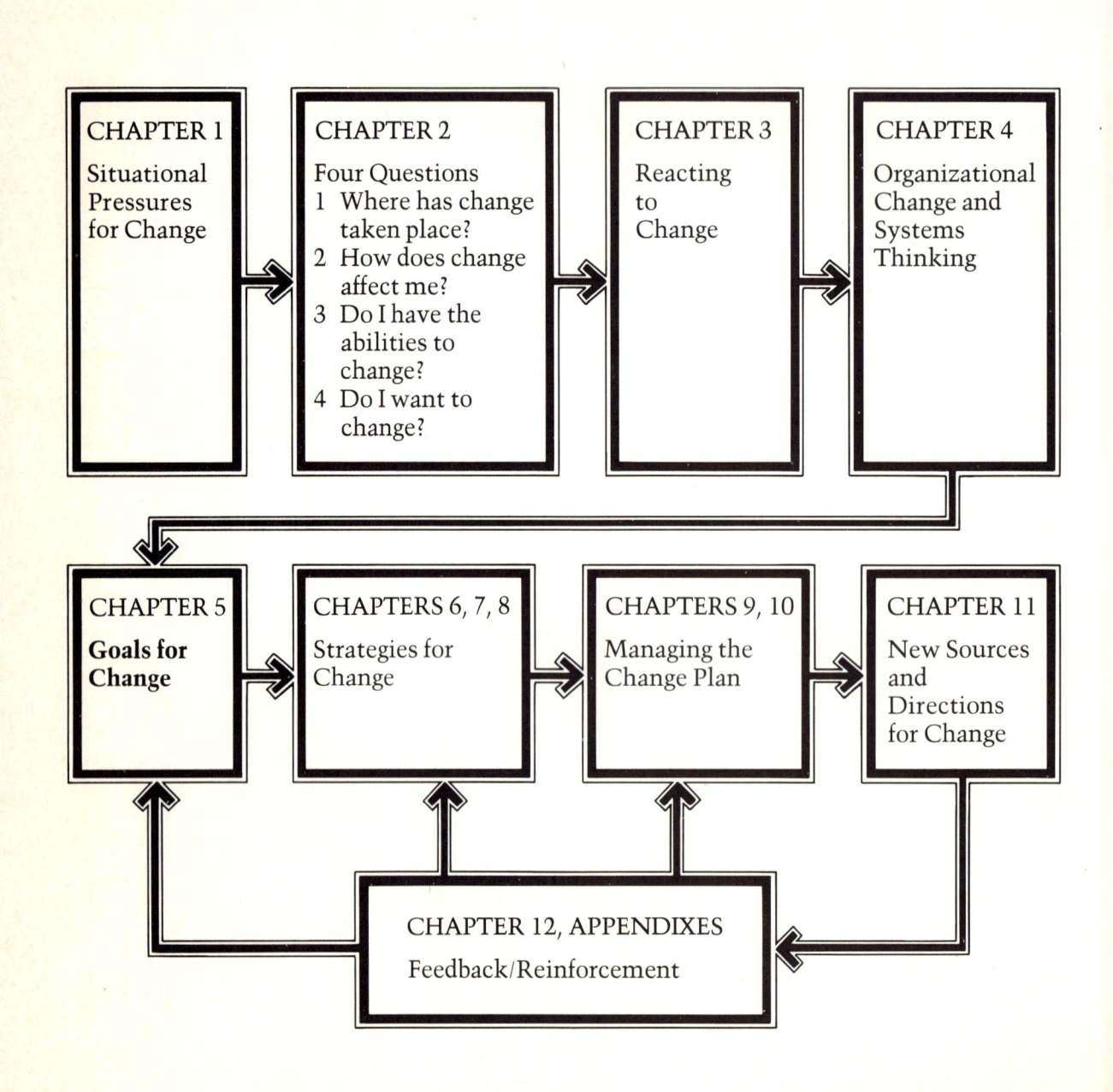

Feedback/Reinforcement

Systems thinking may cause you to question beliefs you previously took for granted and to recognize the need for change in your own attitudes or strategies. (DO I WANT TO CHANGE?) Sometimes through sheer chance we are forced to review our beliefs when we discover how others feel about them (or us). This may be painful. But it can also be beneficial, for change is often initiated by shock effect. The following is a case in point:

Tom Mulligan was convinced that a high rate of turnover in his small auto parts packaging business was due to the types of employees recruited from the neighborhood in which the company was located. The solution he had in mind initially was to find a new area for recruitment, and he was even willing to consider changing his business location.

Quite accidentally, Mulligan got another view of his recruitment problem. One Monday morning, at the drinking fountain in the work area, he overheard two employees discussing his company and his policies. "This outfit is really for the birds," said one of them. "They're only interested in what they can get out of us. And for the least dough possible! Mulligan has forgotten what it's like to be at the other end of things."

Upset by what he heard, Tom Mulligan gave a good deal of thought to his personnel policies. By Friday, he had a growing sense that he had been on the wrong track regarding the reasons for his turnover problem.

Goals Are Problematical

Taking a hard look at a problem sooner or later raises questions about underlying goals. What is it that you actually want to accomplish? The specifics of your goals, along with the way in which they are framed, influence your decisions regarding change.

Systems thinking would have steered Mulligan off the wrong track earlier. When he finally got around to looking at the whole picture, he had to go beyond listening to what others had to say and questioning his stereotypes about people. Finding the source of his problem within rather than outside the organization, he then had to ask himself what kind of an organization he ideally wished to build. If his *goals* included the development of employee commitment, this would entail a longer-term and perhaps costly investment, as opposed to running his business with minimal regard for employee interests.

Goals or Means?

The ability to change is more than the ability to discard old ideas or give up preferred modes of behavior. It is often the ability to look critically at existing goals. This may lead to setting new goals or modifying old ones. Putting it differently, inability to change may be due to unawareness of, lack of clarity about, or opposition to *goals* rather than resistance to *means* to pursue a given goal. Means are only paths to reach objectives, just as trains, buses, or planes are ways to travel to a desired destination.

The possibility for goal attainment is greatly improved through clarification of whether goals, means, or a combination of these are the focus of a problem. In Tom Mulligan's case, moving the plant would have been a change in *means* for reducing turnover, a change that would have contributed little once he reached a different understanding of his goal.

Too *much* change may also result from failure to make this above distinction. When people sarcastically refer to "change for the sake of change," they imply that those they criticize keep changing without regard for goals, or as a substitute for developing meaningful goals.

Whose Goals Are Your Goals?

Confusion between means and goals—which may exist between individuals within an organization or in the thinking of any one person—may in large part be due to difficulties in pinning down objectives. To illustrate this and provide a reference point to return to, put into a few words the goals that give direction to some organizational effort with which you are concerned.

As the kids say, "A sweater is something you wear when your mother is cold." This observation may help you to start thinking about the *source* of your organizational goals.

My organizational goals are:

Goals
connected
with a
particular
project

    _____
    _____
    _____
    _____
    _____

First- and Second-Hand Goals

Each of us is guided by a variety of goals. Some of these are personal and independent of any organizational affiliations. An engineer, for example, may wish to expand his professional knowledge or provide his family with a more comfortable home.

Other goals are tied to a particular organization. The same engineer, a division manager in his company, may have set a goal of improving the design of a long-standing product.

Some goals are set for us. The engineer, for example, may have the responsibility for developing a new product according to rigid specifications.

In the last exercise, whose goals did you write down? Were these goals determined by you? Or, are they organization goals handed down from the top? If the latter is the case, to what extent do these second-hand goals coincide with your own needs, both within and outside the organization? Assessing the overlap between personal and organization goals is important in planning for or understanding reactions to change.

Definite Advantages

How concrete are the goals you just stated? Goals may be couched in general terms, or they may be quite specific. Specific statements are sometimes referred to as *objectives*. The head of a shipping department may, for example, set a goal of filling all orders within two days—or he may set a goal of "maximal efficiency," which could mean gathering a certain group of orders together before shipping—but running the risk of customer delays in receipt.

A business may set a dollar volume to be reached by a stipulated year, or state its goals in terms of "better business in the coming years." A training supervisor may set a goal of five weeks of on-the-job training or specify the specific skills, behaviors, or accuracy to be achieved by the end of that period. The latter is referred to as a *performance-based objective*.

There is nothing wrong with general language. Definite goals, however, have certain advantages. They can be clearly understood by those whom they affect. They also facilitate better organization of resources necessary to their achievement. This makes change more feasible—and its direction more predictable. Definite goals also provide an indisputable means of measuring success and therefore help to confirm or refute the *need* for change.

Being Realistic

A concrete goal is not necessarily a realistic one. In promising shipment within two days, the head of the shipping department may have overestimated the competence of his clerks or underestimated the anticipated volume of business. Access to information is necessary in order to formulate realistic goals. In turn, it is easier to gain support for change when those involved realize that objectives are based on reasonable expectations.

Step by Step

Goals take time to achieve, sometimes quite a long time. Sweeping, far-reaching aspirations are desirable and commendable. But a commitment to posterity, or even to a few years hence, is easier to take casually (thereby delaying change) or even to forget than a goal that specifies what is to be accomplished by next year.

Furthermore, if the goal to be reached by next year is broken down into logical steps along the way, the change for all concerned is less overwhelming. Small changes are more easily conceived and absorbed into ongoing activities. Also the question, DO I HAVE THE ABILITIES TO CHANGE? is less threatening when it is raised as a *series* of questions corresponding to abilities necessary for each step.

The very reluctance to break goals down into manageable parts may represent resistance to change by those who set the goals. In one company, management announced a commitment to developing a profit sharing plan, but a year went by before anything was done to set forth procedures for designing and implementing such a plan. Vagueness, intentional or otherwise, is one way for administrators to prolong taking decisive steps leading to change.

Goals Do Not Stand Alone

Goals may be clearly stated, realistic in terms of the level of competence demanded, and carefully set forth in step form or as objectives. But if they are not compatible with other facets of personal or organizational life, the cards are stacked against achievement. Here is one illustration of the futility of trying to set new goals without regard for the surrounding facts of life.

The main office of a large advertising agency sent Helen Daniels to manage the graphic arts department of a small branch in another state. An atmosphere of informality prevailed in the department, and the work day began with coffee and conversation. After a few weeks, Daniels realized that in reality this period extended well into the morning. Finally comfortable in her new capacity, she called the group together and read the riot act. To her surprise, there was little antagonism and some members indicated that getting down to work was preferable to listless socializing.

Everybody was ready to cooperate in setting a new goal for productive morning work. The only obstacle was that the graphic arts department was highly dependent on work flow originating in other parts of the agency. Without the pressure of actual work before them, there was little impetus for employees to settle down and look for odd jobs. Only interdepartmental coordination could back up the new goal.

The Content of Goals

Several executives, all planning to attend the same seminar on food processing techniques, were asked to state what they expected to achieve. Here are some of the responses:

"In my business it's necessary to keep up with the state of the art."

"I want to meet and keep in contact with others in the field."

"The exchange of ideas will be a source of stimulation."

"My organization needs to maintain its lead in the market."

Note that the first response is phrased in terms of *technical competence;* the second is concerned with *human relationships;* the third focuses on *intellectual processes;* and the fourth is *economic* in emphasis.

Each of these responses may be accepted at face value, that is, as expressive of a primary need related to the technical, social, intellectual, or economic realms. On the other hand, each may just represent a personal bias or habit of mind. People tend to file their thoughts, including their objectives, in favorite or convenient cubbyholes.

The executive who put things in economic terms might readily have conceded that the "exchange of ideas" added up to the same thing. When looking for ways to enlist support for change, it helps to discover which ideas are interchangeable.

Restating Goals

Look back to the goals you stated on p. 57. Are they phrased in technical, social, intellectual, or economic terms?

Now restate what you wrote, drawing on other content areas that express parallel thoughts. As an example, the graphic arts department manager could have set a goal to begin work by 9:30 each morning, stressing the economic value of a working day. A parallel goal could have been to develop more independent habits of work, a goal attuned to human relationships.

Goals expressed in different terms	
Goals as previously stated	_____
Restatements	
Technical	_____
Social relations	_____
Intellectual	_____
Economic	_____

Are any of these restatements more likely to increase your own motivation for change or that of others who are involved? Systems thinking, by taking account of how others view a situation, helps to suggest goal statements in harmony with personal motivations.

Some Troublesome Thoughts

Thinking about goals can be worrysome. On reflection, you may feel that goals are still a complicated matter when you get right down to it. You may be bothered by the fact that goals sometimes *follow* rather than precede means. Indeed, a lot of behavior appears to be random and without goals. We may go along for the ride and then discover a "cause" or something to believe in—a goal. If pressed to state their goals, often people just say what immediately comes to mind, using those convenient mental cubbyholes.

Even more disconcerting is that people sometimes say what they think the other person wants to hear. Politicians excel at this and diplomats are supposed to. But if goals refer to very narrowly defined achievements, they may inhibit flexibility. A salesman charged with opening new accounts, but only those that present *no* economic risk, will be deterred from contacting less established but promising future customers. And when a person holds conflicting goals, change to help achieve one may have negative effects on the other. For example, no matter how clever and experienced, a restaurant owner whose goals are simultaneously to cut costs and improve quality can expect to encounter problems. Conflicting goals may finally lose all power to direct behavior, the sad story behind many business failures.

Goals should provide direction and a general target for accomplishment—with sufficient flexibility to permit the selection of means that can take into account changing circumstances, human differences, and other factors. At the same time they should not be so vague as to provide little or no direction.

It is not easy to separate means from goals, because at some place along the way a goal becomes a means to achieve a higher or different goal. If planning for change includes the establishment of a hierarchy of goals—both long term and immediate—this helps to identify and provide for the necessary sequence of means-ends achievements.

Since means and ends have no fixed definitions, it follows that one person's means may be another person's ends. The means-end distinction, as it relates to the activities of a given individual, helps to reveal the meaning of behavior and to indicate possible directions for change.

Adjusting Goals Along the Way

It would be convenient if goals and means could always be neatly arranged and directly pursued to suit the particular requirements of a change situation. The following case shows that things don't always work out that way. It does suggest that a general sense of purpose or need for change

(DO I WANT TO CHANGE?) allows for flexibility when goals are blocked. Further, gains associated with means to unachieved goals can serve new ends.

Nancy Brown started working as a waitress ten years ago. At first it was just extra income. But when her marriage broke up, working suddenly became a necessity. She always liked the contact with customers but often thought that she would like to take on broader responsibilities, perhaps as a restaurant manager or even an owner. At one time, Brown heard about an opening for a representative with a large insurance broker. She took some crash courses in taxation and business, but the broker considered her background "unrelated." However, the desire to take on added responsibility and gain further independence became even stronger with her.

She changed employers and went to work at a motel restaurant on the outskirts of a large city. After three years, the owner indicated to her he was thinking of retiring. He asked if she would be interested in taking over the restaurant. Brown was very interested. The motel owner indicated that Brown would need to demonstrate her ability to raise working capital for the operation. She would also have to demonstrate the managerial skills necessary to operate a successful restaurant, that is, business abilities, understanding of food operations, and—very important—empathy for the customer. Brown had a series of meetings with the motel owner, his lawyer, and with a bank officer regarding a loan for working capital. With the help of a friend, she also developed a business prospectus, tentative profit-and-loss statements for several years of operation, and a schedule for loan repayment. Brown found that the crash courses taken in the past (means to old goals) and her careful observation of events about her paid off in demonstrating adequate business understanding. Her will to succeed (strong need for **change**), *supported by adequate skills and know-how, appeared to be a model for success.*

Postcript: Brown got the loan, raised her own capital, and bought the restaurant. After more than a year of operation, her business was still growing, not without prob-

lems, but for the most part meeting her business, financial, and management goals.

The Power of Meaningful Goals

One more and very important point on the subject of goals: Once attention is fixed on something we really want to achieve (DO I WANT TO CHANGE?), reality is manipulated to that end. Formerly unacceptable or impossible behavior becomes feasible as sights are adjusted to a particular goal. Such a reversal in attitudes may represent a genuine reappraisal of facts and beliefs as they relate to the newly desired outcome (DO I HAVE THE ABILITIES TO CHANGE?). The reversal may on the other hand be a rationalization in the sense that conflicting elements are forced into harmony with the new goal. In either case, strongly focused behavior tends to be highly selective—to ignore what is inconsistent or fails to be productive, and to assign priority to actions that further progress toward the desired goal. This definitely makes room for change, which is sometimes surprising in magnitude and direction.

Making Goals Work

Meaningful goals are powerful tools for change, but some qualifications are in order.

Examine goals carefully; take them with a grain of salt. The very idea of goals is an oversimplification of both personal and organizational needs and processes. Probe beyond the surface of your own and second-hand goals to discover their relationship to other objectives. Are they authentic goals or are they after-the-fact add ons? If authentic, how might these goals be sharpened or modified to promote support within your organization—*change* in yourself or others?

Careful examination of goals may also lead to their total rejection. This is also desirable change in that it is based on a more sophisticated appreciation of where you and your organization coincide and differ.

The following case history illustrates how individuals in large as well as small organizations can profit from care

Goals for Change

in establishing goals. It illustrates the central theme of this chapter—that awareness of objectives and their interrelationships is imperative if change is to be successful rather than counterproductive.

A midwest concern, manufacturing small motors of excellent quality, enjoyed substantial success for twenty years. On the basis of this many key people within the company believed that the time was right for increasing national distribution.

Much informal discussion finally resulted in a decision by top management to begin seriously planning for the expansion necessary to support wider product distribution. Such expansion was automatically conceived in terms of the construction of additional plants. The focus then shifted to the location of ideal regions and sites and the design of suitable plants for each.

All related planning proceeded in a systematic and thorough manner. Employees were consulted about improvements which, as a result of their experience, should be incorporated in new installations. Activities were undertaken to identify and recruit new candidates for management and sales positions. The training department was given the responsibility for developing a cadre of workers to serve as a core staff for each new plant. Public relations and advertising strategies were also mapped out.

After all these preparations were well under way, it became apparent that the increase and dispersion of production was likely to compromise seriously the firm's ability to continue to produce the superior products that accounted for its present success.

It was necessary at this late point to review the firm's original goal of manufacturing quality equipment. This goal was reaffirmed and, since it was incompatible with plant decentralization, plans for the latter were cancelled. An alternative plan for increasing production through the existing facility was later devised.

Certainly this costly dry run could have been avoided had old and new goals been aired and reconciled much earlier.

In Brief

Examination of any situation demanding change means a critical review of desired achievements. Resistance to change may reflect inappropriate, unclear, or poorly structured goals rather than contrariness or passivity on the part of individuals who are involved.

Goals may be affirmed or rejected through focusing on their sources, meanings, and contradictions. Attainment is more likely when goals are realistic in skill expectations, broken into small and logical sequences, compatible with related constraints, consistent with personal definitions of the need, and sufficiently flexible for creative action.

Stated goals may be misleading in that they often emerge after the fact or as convenient excuses for behavior that has served other purposes. Means are sometimes confused with goals. Individuals may engage in similar activities for different reasons. High motivation to achieve a goal makes for selective behavior (and may also result in compensatory behavior) to support the desired change.

After goals are squarely faced, the time is right to make plans. Discussion of change strategies begins in the following chapter.

Action Checklist

1 Are you aware of your organization's overall goals? Yes ___ No ___

2 Do you know the relative priorities assigned to organizational goals? Yes ___ No ___

3 Can you connect your personal needs or problems with organizational goals? Yes ___ No ___

4 Can you relate organizational goals to change issues primarily associated with your own work situation? Yes ___ No ___

continued

Action Checklist (continued)

5 Have you considered the need for new goals? Yes ___ No ___

6 In responding to multiple goals, are you clear on priorities among them? Yes ___ No ___

7 In dealing with multiple goals, have you dealt adequately with the side effects that are likely to arise? Yes ___ No ___

8 Have you developed a step-by-step plan that is achievable within your time restraints? Yes ___ No ___

9 Will the change criteria be satisfied with respect to *abilities* and *motivation* to change? Yes ___ No ___

Helping Others to Change: External Influences 6

You may have reason to change—or even to change those higher up.

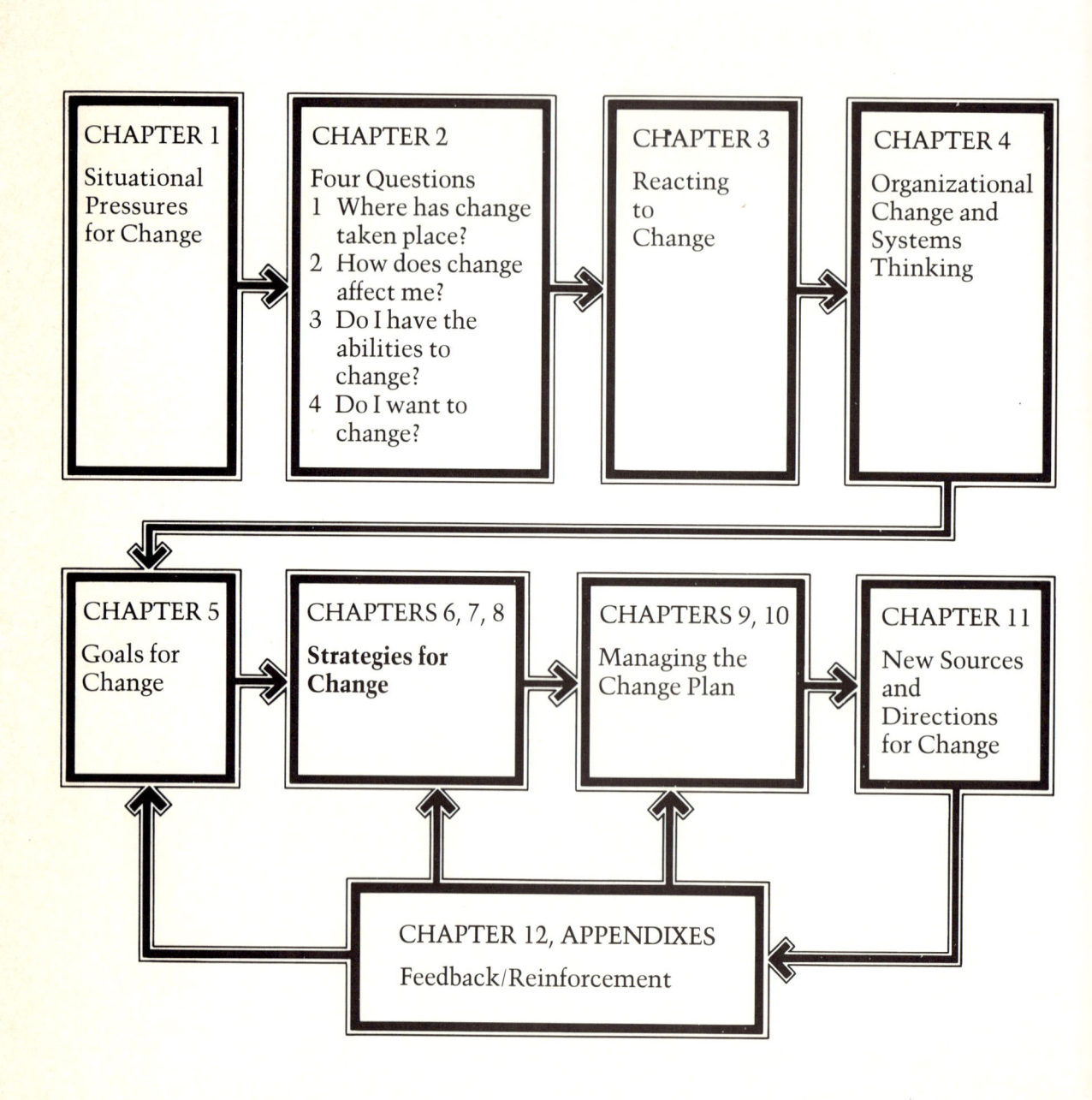

CHAPTER 1	CHAPTER 2	CHAPTER 3	CHAPTER 4
Situational Pressures for Change	Four Questions 1 Where has change taken place? 2 How does change affect me? 3 Do I have the abilities to change? 4 Do I want to change?	Reacting to Change	Organizational Change and Systems Thinking

CHAPTER 5	CHAPTERS 6, 7, 8	CHAPTERS 9, 10	CHAPTER 11
Goals for Change	**Strategies for Change**	Managing the Change Plan	New Sources and Directions for Change

CHAPTER 12, APPENDIXES

Feedback/Reinforcement

Clarification of goals is an important step wherever personal or organizational change is concerned. We will now examine a classification and discussion of ways for you to help others change once you have established those goals. The discussion is not limited to individuals with direct management responsibilities. The need for change may be anywhere in an organization, and change can flow in any direction. You may have reason to change or offer suggestions for change to fellow workers, to work change through those you report to, or even to change those higher up. The latter is not impossible to accomplish.

In addition to place of work, most of us function within several organizations of some type—professional, civic, social, recreational, and family, to name just a few. Becoming more familiar with ways to promote change will help you to make better use of what you already know, as well as adding to your repertoire of approaches. It will also increase your ability to extend help to friends or associates who may be struggling with change-related problems.

Means Are Neutral

Methods or means for promoting change are neither good nor bad in themselves. As ways to exert influence, they may be used to serve the worst or the most noble purposes. These methods are not foolproof, since influence does not always work as intended, for reasons that will later become clear. Nor are they all equally feasible and appropriate in a given situation.

Both the nature of the demands and the readiness of persons to change affect the selection of change strategies. Before selecting means to further a particular change it is important to assess where others stand on the same questions you asked yourself earlier.

- Do they know where change has occurred?

- Do they realize how change will affect them?

- Do they have the abilities to change?

- Do they want to change?

Changing People or Circumstances?

You can change circumstances to help people change. Or you can make a more direct attempt to change people. This chapter focuses on changing the *circumstances* in which people find themselves; the next chapter deals with the second approach.

By circumstances we mean that which is external and not directly subject to an individual's control. Circumstances may include responsibilities as defined by others, organizational rules and regulations, the physical environment in terms of place or equipment, and the social environment in terms of the number, characteristics, and activities of others who share the environment.

Some changes in circumstances may seem inconsequential, yet the effects may be substantial. A new budget, a revised auditing system, or an impersonal inquiry regarding procedures may all set in motion changes in an individual's behavior. The very presence—or even the rumor—of a new executive may change attitudes toward work or the organization (especially if you had figured on getting the job!). Note that these instances represent events originating "out there" in the organization's environment (WHERE HAS CHANGE TAKEN PLACE?) rather than within or initiated by the persons they affect.

Which Comes First?

A distinction between people and circumstances is always somewhat artificial because people affect circumstances and vice versa. In fact, this give and take is the ideal end product, but it may be more readily achieved by concentrating in one direction rather than another.

For example, suppose that a desired change is to increase employee participation in training opportunities (such as adult education courses) within a community. Would it be easier for employees to take advantage of these opportunities if the company altered working conditions or *circumstances*—say by allowing time off the job for training purposes or contributing to the cost of tuition? Or, should direct efforts be made to raise the ambitions or aspirations of employees—to *change the person*—perhaps through individual interviews and counseling? If so, how effective would this be without more flexibility in working hours, subsidizing tuition, and so on?

By all means work out a strategy combining both approaches whenever this is possible. One answer, when a choice must be made, however, recently came from the owner of a small-town variety store. This man remarked that it is amazing how thoughtful people become when he puts greeting cards on sale! He well realized that it isn't always necessary to work on the character or temperament of people to modify their behavior.

Common to whether an attempt is made to change the person and/or the circumstances is a belief in the desire and ability of a human being to change. The particular argument in favor of the circumstances approach rests on the notion that people are storehouses for a great variety of possible responses. To cope with new realities, an individual need not change in some basic way, but instead draws from a stock of alternative capacities. In the greeting card example, the new reality (a bargain) created an opportunity to produce a stored response (thoughtfulness).

Changing the Circumstances

There are various ways within organizations to tap potential responses. In the following methods to be discussed, the accent is on changing circumstances rather than overhauling the individual, but remember that the distinction is not to be pressed to the wall:

HAT CHANGING

ENVIRONMENT CHANGING

MESSAGES

REWARD AND PUNISHMENT

Hat Changing

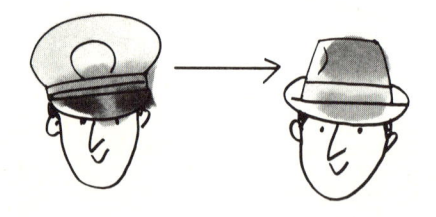

Both in the course of a life and in the course of a single day, most of us play several roles. A role is the set of duties and expectations connected with a particular status or position in some set of relationships. Words like boss, grandfather, teacher, oldest child, and host each suggest different responsibilities and privileges.

A Role Specifies Behavior

As in a play, a role specifies how to behave. There is of course more leeway in real roles. And, unlike a play, real life roles are not make-believe. Each of the many parts portrayed is a real aspect of the self. Or, it might be said that each of us has many selves. These selves are often surprisingly unlike and sometimes so contradictory that great pains must be taken to avoid "performing" or letting ourselves *show* before the wrong audience. The dominating boss but henpecked husband is a case in point.

This capacity to play diverse roles illustrates that the elements are always present within an individual for different forms of behavior. Hat changing or assignment to new roles brings change at one level by demanding another kind of *performance*.

Change is not restricted to mere performance, however. A deeper basis for change develops as the "actor" begins to see the world through the new role or status. The recently promoted and overbearing supervisor may be accused by his former buddies of having forgotten what it means to work on the line, but there is more to it than that. Some of the new supervisor's changed behavior can be explained by what is actually expected of him as a supervisor—together with the change in outlook brought about by an altered relationship to the system in which he works.

Examples of Hat Changing

Hat changing in organizations ordinarily takes place through promotion or reassignment, although the intent may seldom be to change the person. In fact, the very ability of a person to change hats is often the basis for promotion. This is frequently interpreted as a demonstration of individual flexibility. The ability to see things another way is sometimes consciously fostered through temporary hat changing or assignment to a job or series of jobs for a brief period. Many companies incorporate such experiences in their training programs.

Another type of temporary hat changing is *role playing*. In this procedure, members of an organization come together to take the parts of others while focusing on specific organizational issues. The purpose may be to extend knowledge of the factors relevant to a situation, to correct misconceptions, to resolve some conflict, or to develop new skills through the performance of a role. Some typical situations to which role playing has been applied are anticipation of consumer response to a new product, introduction of women or racial minorities into management, threat of a company to leave town because of environmental controls or the possibilities of new enforcement levels, and difficulties in resolving scheduling or delivery problems between sales and production. Whatever the reasons for using this approach, change in perspective, understanding, and/or activity is the anticipated outcome.

How to Role Play The following steps outline the role playing process:

1 *An introductory statement* is drafted that states the purpose of the role play and the nature of the problem or situation to be discussed.

2 *A setting* is named, such as a council meeting, sales meeting, interview, or whatever seems to be typical of the issue.

3 *Roles are developed.* The number and type are determined by the situation. For example, there may be an interviewer and interviewee, members of production and sales staffs, a store manager and hypothetical customer. Each person designated to play a role is given a short description of the role (position, responsibility, age and sex if appropriate, and so on). Each must play his or her role as realistically as possible—as that actual person would ordinarily respond to the situation or events.

4 *Roles are played out.* This may last from fifteen minutes to a half hour or longer. The situation is natural to the extent that if the setting is a board meeting, the chairperson presides. A moderator, such as a trainer or senior manager, assumes the responsibility for redirecting the role play if it gets off target.

5 *Review and critique.* This is provided by the moderator. At times, a small panel is formed with additional people to round out the information fed back to the role participants—how well roles were played, problems that surfaced, leadership style, problem solution, and so on.

6 *Rotation of roles.* Roles are often rotated among participants to expose each of them to another viewpoint. This is especially valuable in sex and race issues.

Role Difficulties Important as it is to develop an appreciation for how roles channel behavior, it would be naive to assume that people slip into new roles all that easily or that role specifications are always that cut and dried. Role specifications vary greatly, ranging from extremely rigid job descriptions to reliance on diffuse terms such as "executive" to denote what is expected of the person assuming the role. Usually the more complex the role, the more latitude there is for bringing personal definitions to bear on performance. Note the ongoing efforts to define the proper scope of the American presidency.

Bearing in mind these limitations, role assignment provides a valuable way to induce change. And one of the limitations, namely the looseness of definitions for some roles, is a powerful force for *unplanned* change—in that people supply their own definitions.

A good example of this situation is found in the following example:

Pat Herman was sales manager for a division of a consumer products company. The firm had always been run loosely in the past with the idea that "independence" helped to develop people. Although business situations and sales strategies became increasingly complex with intense competition, few policy changes were made in the company. Pat Herman was an independent person and felt he had a good command of his territory and could handle things. When he learned that a competitor was about to come out with a newer product, he decided quick action was necessary. He took it upon himself to authorize a change in product specifications for an existing company item to deal with the new competition. The revised product did in fact do an excellent job in meeting the new competitive product. Unfortunately, it also raised Herman's company's costs by 40 percent.

In this example, an individual supplied an important definition of his job that included "authority for making product change." After all, he had never been told he didn't have such authority. This action turned out to be an extremely costly lesson for the company concerned; it subsequently sparked a dramatic revision of management responsibilities, a change long overdue.

Current Roles

To get a better feeling for what roles are all about, stop at this point and list the roles you have played—within and outside your organization—in the last two days:

_____
_____
_____

Are you one person as a boss, another with friends, and still another as a parent? Does your ability to be many and different people surprise even you?

How much do your own definitions bear on each role? If you believe, for instance, that managers have a duty to keep their subordinates informed on company matters, how does this affect the actions you take?

Do you have some currently underused traits or skills that you feel are likely to be valued by others? For example, you may write well, have an excellent memory for facts and figures, or be a "born diplomat." Could an opportunity to express these qualities in a new role lead to some significant change in your life? If, for instance, your talents for diplomacy were put into service, such as public relations or interdepartmental liaison, would you learn more, develop greater self-confidence, or become more valuable and visible to your company?

Environment Changing

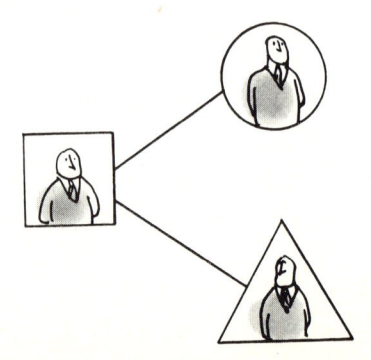

When a difficult child is enrolled in a new school or an unsuccessful salesman is transferred to a different territory, there is tacit assumption that the environment will present fresh opportunities for accomplishment and that the individual has the qualities necessary to respond constructively (DO I HAVE THE ABILITIES TO CHANGE?). Individual change may be promoted in this manner without modifying basic responsibilities. That is, the person remains in the role of student or salesman as the case might be.

New Inputs

The aim in shifting surroundings is to take advantage of human factors that are known to be somewhat or altogether different in the new setting. The idea is that environmental change will foster personal change through the values, experiences, role definitions, and so forth of changed associates and circumstances. Due credit must be given also to the part played by physical surroundings. Sunshine, clean air, quiet rural life, or glamorous city life have all been known to work wonders.

Organizational Approaches

Organizations make extensive use of transfer, either utilizing the transferred person to impose change on others, or, as described above, to encourage change in the person transferred. Change of environment may also be arranged on a short-term basis, such as temporary assignment to another branch. In some organizations it is regular policy to transfer managerial personnel, both for purposes of individual development and to prevent the organization itself from becoming too channelized in procedures or certain directions. Such organizations are in fact placing positive value on change by not allowing their people to assume rigid routine sets of behavior—by keeping people flexible in their thinking and approaches. (As an aside, too much change can be disruptive; a sensible middle ground must be established.)

Other types of environment change include participation in a retreat (often at a plush resort), meeting locally off the premises with associates (the bar at a downtown hotel may substitute for the resort), or meeting in a spot on company premises away from the usual place of operations. None of these arrangements shift roles within the organization; they do provide a different atmosphere in which to discuss pressing issues and often to come into contact with outsiders having parallel responsibilities. The latter is often considered the most important factor for those attending professional meetings where peers meet and talk shop. Even when there is no change of associates, the novel setting and freedom from everyday pressure allow for new combinations of ideas and behaviors and, occasionally, a safe place to try them out.

Hidden Possibilities

As with role change, environmental change may lead to many different results. Some may be surprising or even work *too* well. The famous song from World War I immortalized the latter problem: "How you gonna keep 'em down on the farm after they've seen Paree?"

Change Resulting from New Environment

Consider the influence of environment on your own life. Think of an instance where a new or modified environment changed your work performance. Describe specifically what the new situation contributed to cause you to change. Enter a situation or two in the following table:

Type of environment	Type of change	Reasons
___	___	___
___	___	___
___	___	___
___	___	___

Could you have predicted the effects?

Messages

The warning that appears on a pack of cigarettes is meant to convey information that may change your mind about smoking. The message is strong in tone, but it doesn't tell you what to do. The purpose, supposedly, is to inform you about what you may not already know (WHERE HAS CHANGE TAKEN PLACE?) in the hope or belief that ignorance alone is the cause of your present behavior.

Working on the same assumptions, positively as well as negatively worded messages come our way in the form of campaign literature, television commercials, newspaper ads, conversations with friends, and so on. Organizations, too, circulate information with the aim of changing people. Beyond the routine procedure of informing, many of those memos, reports, charts, and the like carry a sometimes subtle, but forceful message to modify the status quo.

Get the Message?

Although information may be accurate and well-intentioned, it often fails to accomplish the desired results. Under what conditions is a message likely to work or be ignored?

Bombarded as we all are by countless communications and competing stimuli, messages are most likely to get through when they fit with what we need, what we believe, or what we are ready to do anyway (here, simply acting as a cue). The message that captures attention may provide new information or just confirm what is already known. It may suggest a fresh approach or simply bolster confidence in a potential decision. Messages may serve also to reinforce the wisdom of past decisions.

In brief, messages that are nonthreatening or consistent with the direction of change in which the receiver may be traveling are more likely to be heeded. But for the same reasons such messages sometimes contribute only minimally to the change process. Some threatening messages (such as legal action for nonpayment of a bill) also get results. This will be discussed shortly. For now, we will only examine messages where real choices exist for the receiver.

New and Shocking Messages As all advertising experts know, novelty is effective for capturing attention. The same is true for shock effect. If there is a nagging discrepancy between what you believe and a message that does not support that belief, the conditions may be ripe for change. You may recall from the preceding chapter that the owner of a business was highly disturbed, but constructively motivated for action, when he overheard employees criticizing him for insensitivity and exploitation.

An example of this type of situation occurred at a paper carton plant.

Mel Lasnover, the plant superintendent, was convinced that his production line was operating at top efficiency despite complaints from the sales department that costs were too high. Lasnover's conviction was shaken at a meeting of a paper carton manufacturers association. While talking shop with another plant manager, he learned that the other manager's costs of production of a popular-sized carton were 20 percent less than his. The lower cost was confirmed by a manager from a third plant. At this point, Lasnover started wondering about his costs of producing this standard size carton. He wondered about costs of other sizes as well.

An effective but different kind of shock comes from a message revealing that the alternatives to the intended change are even worse. The parents who can't accept a prospective son-in-law of the "wrong" religion may change their minds in a hurry on learning that their daughter is pregnant!

Says Who?   The *source* of the message also affects receptivity to its content. In general, we are more influenced by those in our immediate environment than by remote or impersonal figures. Within the immediate environment the messages of respected or powerful friends, colleagues, or authorities are the most convincing. Such individuals often serve to receive and distribute messages from more distant authorities. This enhances the credibility of the latter and exerts important social pressure to accept the message.

Beneath and Beyond the Message

The big problem with messages, regardless of who conveys them, is that behavior is determined by more than just rational considerations or by what seems sensible to the message sender. From the underlying reasons for resistance to change discussed in Chapter 3, it can be seen that some information conveys a "message" that is completely unintended. A communication outlining plans for company reorganization may cause some employees to question the organization's stability and begin to look for work elsewhere, rather than accept the positive implications intended by the message. We don't suggest withholding useful information, but don't count on it to produce miracles.

Saying It Another Way

On the other hand, people can be helped to change without necessarily overcoming certain resistances. We often liberate ourselves—and this need not be self-deceit or hypocrisy—by simply changing, on the basis of new evidence or conclusion, the way we classify or categorize a situation. Resistance to a luxurious purchase, for example, may cease when the purchase is redefined as a hedge against inflation. In that case the resisting individual need not alter a conservative self-image. To take another example, delegation of authority may become permissible when preservation of health is defined as the critical need of the person delegating the authority. This does not require any permanent revision of leadership philosophy on the part of the delegator. Redefinition is more a means for bypassing rather than dissolving resistance.

Another possibility for change related to redefining a situation occurs when you make a commitment to do something (define the situation as sufficiently binding—DO I WANT TO CHANGE?) and then follow through on the basis of the commitment. The resulting behavior initially may have little to do with basic beliefs and wishes, yet once accepted the contract is honored, so to speak. This is a familiar enough mechanism that operates in everyday life to produce change. A reluctantly but dutifully accepted blind date may turn a confirmed bachelor into a husband, or a pressured financial pledge to some charitable organization may lead to serious work for its cause. The trick is to get some type of commitment through an effective message and then hope for the best—on the basis that even a grudging commitment opens the door to change.

What's in a Good Message?

Doubtless you receive your share of messages, many of which contain important and well-meaning information. Choose a successful message, one on which you have acted, and analyze what it had going for it.

Elements of a successful message _____
_____
_____
_____
_____

Check it on the following points:

☐ Corresponds with a personal need or belief
☐ Your prior readiness to act on the message

continued

What's in a Good Message? (continued)

- ☐ Novelty of presentation
- ☐ Shock value
- ☐ Respectability of the source
- ☐ New definition of a situation previously resisted
- ☐ Ability to secure a commitment from you

Reward and Punishment

Some messages seeking to bring about change in performance are backed up by more than words. Tangible rewards and punishments may be set forth, corresponding to acceptable or nonacceptable behavior.

In organizational life, rewards may take material or nonmaterial form, ranging from simple recognition to elaborate testimonial dinners, and from prizes, salary increases, and bonuses to gaining a share of ownership. By definition, promotions are rewards—at least there is a face value.

Short of demotion, punishment in organizations may be more subtle in that the message must be read between the lines. Nevertheless, there is no lack of techniques or descriptive vocabulary. People are "kicked upstairs," allowed to "cool their heels," transferred to "the sticks," and "passed over" in terms of promotion and raises.

Gold Stars or Gold?

Offhand, it would seem that rewards and punishment almost guarantee desired results, especially if the stakes are known in advance. The chances are certainly better if rewards are interpreted as appropriate or desirable to all concerned. How many of us really cared about gold stars for good spelling? Would candy bars have been more interesting? (Clearly, some dentists would have favored this reward.) Although it is true that some people go along with gold stars, especially if they feel this eventually leads to better things, others are not so eager or farsighted. If rewards are to work as true incentives to change, they deserve careful thought in relation to the value system of the target group. In addition, rewards should be possible to accept. A long and distant trip might be highly desirable but completely unrealistic as a reward for a person with young children.

Pros and Cons of Coercion

With punishment the picture is more complicated. You are probably familiar with the controversy as to whether it is possible to legislate compliance. Compliance may refer to equal opportunity, environmental, or criminal issues. It is argued, first, that legislation creates a new reality that must (under threat of punishment) be responded to. Second, once there is acceptance of this (HOW DOES CHANGE AFFECT ME!)—the intended responses obtained—compliance tends to be accompanied by more basic change. If an employer strongly opposed to female employment is forced to hire women, for example, he may discover their value to his firm. This is another example of an environmental change, described earlier.

The argument may be reversed. The compliant but opposed employer may sustain his beliefs about women (DO I WANT TO CHANGE?) by continuing to observe only what fits those beliefs or by treating women in such a manner that they cannot help but prove him right.

Helping Others to Change

There is evidence to support both arguments. Laws or direct orders from the boss will usually produce outward compliance, even if in some cases there is only surface change. For example, a penalty for plant safety violations may be reasonably effective without changing actual attitudes toward safety. If genuine cooperation is the goal, it would be wiser to encourage change through additional or alternative methods.

Time sometimes runs out, however, and last resort measures may be necessary to produce change. This was the case for a large chain of retail food stores that went to great lengths to prepare their managers for enlightened compliance with equal opportunity regulations. When it became clear that many managers were still failing to meet their new responsibilities, top management announced that salary increases and promotions were to be evaluated in terms of managers' support of the program. To further ensure change, it was stated that failure to comply would be grounds for dismissal.

But even forced change is not simply coercion if there are elements within a situation that are compatible with the new requirements. For instance, mandatory compliance with a new office procedure will meet with voluntary compliance if those who must follow the new system have the necessary skills to deal with it (DO I HAVE THE ABILITIES TO CHANGE?) and if the system itself proves useful to them. For example, acceptance of computer-based systems is likely to be greater if affected employees can make sense of computer printouts.

The Quality of Change

Some may argue that, in many respects, life is simplified by straight orders (messages) that define the limits of behavior. True, a KEEP OFF THE GRASS sign may do the job—but even then maybe only when someone is watching. When change calls for a more willing or creative contribution it is still advisable to send *rewarding* messages.

Rewards Motivating Change

Consider the impact and value of material and nonmaterial rewards in your own life. Then list some material and nonmaterial rewards that have motivated you to change.

Rewards that counted

Material
_____
_____
_____

Nonmaterial
_____
_____
_____

Do you feel these rewards are equally important for others?

Promoting Change Through External Factors

Indicate in the table below whether you are able to introduce the following possibilities (that is, to change working circumstances) in a particular situation calling for change—and how important you think the strategy might be.

	DEGREE OF PERSONAL INFLUENCE			DEGREE OF IMPORTANCE		
	Low	Some	High	Low	Some	High
Job Assignment						
Transfer						
Promotion or different job						
Temporary transfer						

continued

Promoting Change Through External Factors (continued)

	DEGREE OF PERSONAL INFLUENCE			DEGREE OF IMPORTANCE		
	Low	Some	High	Low	Some	High
Temporary Changes of Environment						
Meeting sites						
Retreats						
Informal settings						
Work Responsibilities						
Scope						
Depth						
Clientele, people contacted						
Communications						
Media selection						
Development of communications						
Frequency						
Sanctions and Rewards						
Monetary rewards						
Nonmonetary rewards						
Direct punishment						
Implied punishment						

continued

Promoting Change Through External Factors (continued)

	DEGREE OF PERSONAL INFLUENCE			DEGREE OF IMPORTANCE		
	Low	Some	High	Low	Some	High
Methods, Procedures						
Working Conditions						
Physical						
Hours						
Policies						

In Brief

People may be encouraged to change by altering the circumstances or reality to which they must respond or by attempting more directly to modify their personal characteristics and inclinations. Measures associated with the first approach include:

Hat changing	new responsibilities through new roles
Environment changing	change of locale and all that includes
Messages	circulation of information in various forms and contexts
Reward and punishment	messages with strings attached

These strategies cut across each other. The distinctions are merely a convenience for highlighting central ideas and for making it simpler to review them for future application.

Action Checklist

1 Do you understand what is meant by helping people to change by modifying the circumstances affecting them—in contrast to attempting to change people in more direct fashion? Yes ____ No ____

2 Role playing is sometimes used for deep-seated problems involving attitudes or understanding. Can you visualize places where this approach might be applied advantageously? Yes ____ No ____

3 Can you develop a workable list of environment-related strategies that your organization could use to promote change? Yes ____ No ____

4 Can you identify points in your own career development where modifications of environment affected your work performance? Yes ____ No ____

5 Have you considered the relative effectiveness of various media, messages, and sources as vehicles for change? Yes ____ No ____

6 Can you determine what types of rewards would best relate to the values of group members in a particular situation calling for change? Yes ____ No ____

Helping Others: Leaders as Models for Change 7

From infancy we pattern our lives after examples set by those who mean most to us.

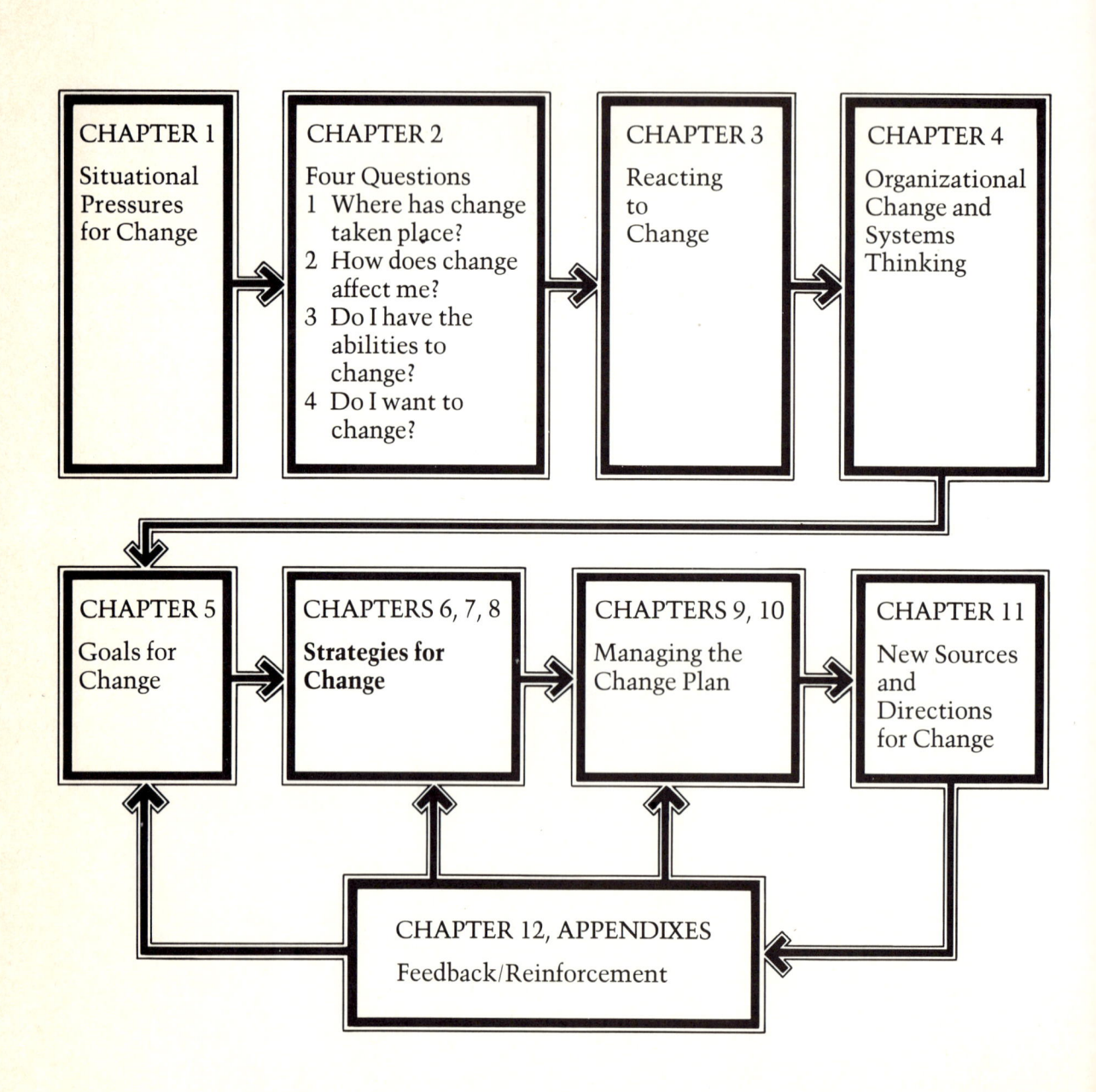

CHAPTER 1	CHAPTER 2	CHAPTER 3	CHAPTER 4
Situational Pressures for Change	Four Questions 1 Where has change taken place? 2 How does change affect me? 3 Do I have the abilities to change? 4 Do I want to change?	Reacting to Change	Organizational Change and Systems Thinking

CHAPTER 5	CHAPTERS 6, 7, 8	CHAPTERS 9, 10	CHAPTER 11
Goals for Change	**Strategies for Change**	Managing the Change Plan	New Sources and Directions for Change

CHAPTER 12, APPENDIXES

Feedback/Reinforcement

The last chapter discussed changing the circumstances or *external conditions* to which a person responds. This chapter is about more direct ways of changing the person. The latter part of the chapter takes up the question of how to work out a plan making use of both types of strategies. A chart will be introduced to simplify the suggested procedure for determining and weighing the possibilities available under various sets of conditions.

Whether nagging or patiently explaining, parents and teachers spend much time and effort on people-changing strategies. They use (or attempt to use) their influence to bring about basic change in personality itself, as well as behavior. Here we look at some of the ways in which this type of change is fostered in young and old alike:

FRIENDSHIP, ADMIRATION, RESPECT

TRAINING AND DEVELOPMENT (NONTECHNICAL)

TECHNICAL TRAINING

Friendship, Admiration, Respect

From infancy, we pattern our lives after the examples set by those who mean most to us. There is need both to be like these important figures and to win their approval (DO I WANT TO CHANGE?). What begins as simple conformity or identification with another person gradually becomes a more genuine aspect of one's own personality—change that is more than skin deep. The saying, "The apple doesn't fall very far from the tree," sums up this complex process as it operates between parents and children. The process extends throughout life to other important relationships such as between an individual and supervisor, friend, or other person who acts as a desirable model for one's own behavior. Within an organization, these bonds are an ongoing force for change.

Leaders as Models for Change

In Chapter 6 we pointed out that messages are most likely to be heeded when their source is powerful or respected. Those in an organization who have earned the esteem of others are also more likely to act as models for thought and behavior. Respected individuals can thus send very *personal* messages (HOW DOES CHANGE AFFECT ME?).

This is an opportunity too often overlooked in organizational planning for change. Respect and admiration cannot be artificially manufactured—"earned" is indeed the right word in connection with such sentiments. It follows that individuals who have the respect of others should be sought out to pave the way for change or to ease people through the trauma accompanying change.

The ability to inspire special regard is operative throughout an organization. It cuts across formal authority. Friendship groups are an important source of direct or personal influence. As in the family, sustained day-to-day contact (in work groups, within departments, and so on) often creates common ties and a need for good standing within the group. As a result of shared activities, problems, and corresponding feelings of camaraderie and mutual dependence, such groups develop their own informal rules and goals. The messages their members send to each other may either complement or resist organizational objectives.

To describe this influence as pressure is not quite accurate. What takes place in cohesive groups is more fundamental and voluntary in nature. There is constant opportunity to exchange and assess views with respected coworkers. Trust allows people to let their hair down. A less defensive attitude means openness to change. Seen in this light, human relationships in a work context are a resource for bringing about change.

The Role of Management

The role of management also deserves special comment. Either through default or choice, higher management is often invisible to large numbers of organization members. Sometimes a decision is made to avoid direct interaction with those at lower levels in the belief that this will better protect managerial objectivity and the freedom or creativity of subordinates. Whatever the reasons, management that is aloof, and therefore unknown, cannot exercise leadership or serve as inspiration (model for behavior) in the direct sense we have been discussing. Such management is at a disadvantage in promoting change and may even increase resistance to change owing to the tendency to regard the unfamiliar with suspicion. There is much to be gained when management personnel are not afraid to present themselves as real and at times vulnerable human beings. Where management moves beyond this to participate actively with those at lower levels in efforts connected with change, the impact is even more personal in its effects.

Work Relationships that Have Influenced Personal Beliefs

Quite apart from the ability to bring us into line, both fellow workers and superiors have the power to shape (change) thinking. Are you able to verify this with examples from your own experience? Give at least three examples of work relationships that caused a change in your thinking or beliefs.

Relationship	Change in beliefs

Are the forces of friendship, admiration, and respect sufficiently understood in your organization? These can be powerful change forces.

Training and Development

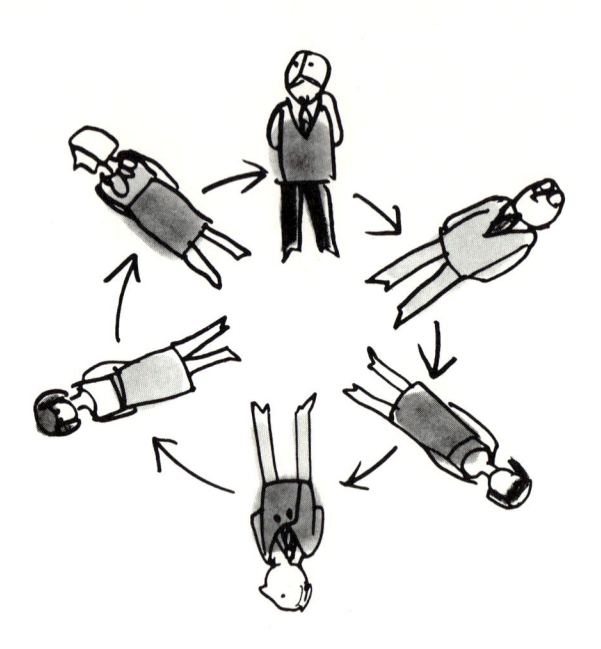

Laboratory training, management training, sensitivity training, and other types of nontechnical training are familiar enough these days. In all probability you have experienced some of these activities firsthand. Although these trainings differ in many respects, their basic purpose is to improve organizational functioning through greater awareness of human needs and social processes. This implies fundamental change. These types of training tend to take one of two directions: (1) *self-development,* which is in greatest use, and which seeks to build skills or further self-knowledge (for fuller experience and harmony with others); (2) *organizational development,* which focuses on the underlying work and social processes of organizations. Organization Development, as a special field, is the subject of the next chapter.

When and What

Training and development may be undertaken as an aspect of general organizational development or at times as a response to a crisis situation. Leadership may be relatively loose or unstructured or lean toward more traditional structured approaches. The choice of individual or group training activity appropriate to organizational needs requires professional assistance. Specifics of the approach are determined by the answers to various key questions such as: Are the objectives short or long range? Are they conceived in terms of prevention or troubleshooting? Is it the desire to improve management skills or general human functioning?

All such forms of activity involve, to a greater or lesser degree, coworkers of the work group as stimuli to learning. Through their interactions, members cause each other to examine their responses to situations of mutual concern. Even when concentration is primarily on self-development (rather than skill training), questions concerning policy, work organization, and technology are typically discussed as underlying or contributing factors. These subjects may come up in more earthy form such as the understood rules and regulations, or dos and don'ts to preserve harmony.

There is special emphasis in such training on learning to listen and to communicate ideas and feelings more effectively. This includes the expression of conflict—the constructive clash of ideas.

Conflict Because conflict is usually equated with trouble and tends to make us uncomfortable, we generally avoid rather than encourage it. The negative side of conflict is well known, but there is also a positive side that relates to change. Conflict can be viewed as a normal outgrowth of individual differences, vested interests, or simply the inevitable frictions that arise when people live or work together. An opportunity to blow off steam is important in that it keeps anger from interfering with normal functioning and from accumulating to explosive points. But conflict that can be "managed" may serve other highly useful functions. Managed conflict brings suppressed ideas, frustrations, and arguments to the surface, which increases the possibilities for new solutions. Getting things out into the open clears the way for new sets of relationships among the parties to the conflict, which also serves to promote change. Above all, managed conflict can keep people in the organization involved, striving for some progress. This is much more productive than the alternatives—anger and apathy.

An example in an executive's office helps to bring out this matter of conflict resolution and change.

Fred Bekels was vice president for finance of a small automotive supply firm. He had often been at odds with the vice president of production, A. J. Trask, over production's seeming disregard for the costs of scrap. After one particular production run that resulted in much costly scrap, Bekels confronted Trask and demanded an explanation. He was told in no uncertain terms that it was none of his business. A heated discussion arose between the two men, one that lasted until the early evening. At last, both were exhausted. Yet somehow they both felt better. They had gotten things out on the table that had long been bothering both of them. Out of their knock-down, dragout, a new mutual understanding arose of purpose, responsibility, and means of discharging these.

Managing Conflict as a Change Strategy It follows that conflict is not only a natural but important part of organizational life. It doesn't simply happen; rather, it has assignable causes. If it is dealt with thoughtfully, conflict can be a powerful factor in catalyzing change.* If ignored or mishandled, it can create major problems.

Conflict management depends on identification of the sources of conflict and a careful approach to their resolution. In general, there are three types of conflict. A checklist on pp. 101–2 suggests ways of identifying these.

The manner of dealing with these three types of conflict varies considerably. Conflict due to mis-communications or omissions in communications is prob-

---

* For more details and references, see William C. Morris and Marshall Sashkin, *Organization Behavior in Action: Skill Building Exercises* (St. Paul, Minn.: West Publishing Co., 1972), pp. 201–5.

ably dealt with most easily, although unless a deliberate effort is made it is often quite difficult to detect this source of trouble. Good knowledge of communication can minimize this type of conflict.

Managing conflict for change where "facts" are involved is usually handled through establishing the validity of currently available information and/or researching for new ideas. However, the seasoned manager recognizes that facts can be interpreted to suit a variety of purposes. Thus, getting people to relinquish one set of facts in favor of another may not be easy, although this is essential if new directions are called for.

Where considerable emotion or deep-seated values underlie conflict, the person seeking to introduce change is faced with a major challenge. Role play as a change technique is an effective technique in dealing with this type of conflict.

At times, because of legislative requirements, time, or other priorities, you may be forced to demand the necessary change (as in equal employment compliance). Clearly, this is an unsatisfactory means for dealing with conflict. The individuals involved cannot be ignored, and it is the prudent manager who undertakes some type of longer term educational effort.

Sources of Conflict

Conflict Due to Misunderstanding or Miscommunication

1 Do the parties to the situation have a clear understanding of what is involved? Yes____ No____

2 Have terms or ideas been used that are likely to be misunderstood? Yes____ No____

3 Have people been asked for feedback to assure common understanding? Yes____ No____

4 Have media (letters, bulletins, memos), been selected that minimize misunderstanding? Yes____ No____

continued

Sources of Conflict (continued)

Conflict Due to Legitimate or Factual Matters

5 Do the parties to the conflict possess documentation/incidents supporting their position?   Yes ____ No ____

6 Is precedent or policy cited as a basis for the positions taken?   Yes ____ No ____

7 Has the work, reports, or analyses of other departments/groups been introduced as a basis for the conflict?   Yes ____ No ____

8 Has there been a validation of the information cited that assures its accuracy and timeliness?   Yes ____ No ____

Conflict Due to Differences in Importance or Value Assigned

9 Is it clear that people are stating their opinion as to the issues involved?   Yes ____ No ____

10 Are people drawing on personal values in judging the relative merits or importance of the issues involved?   Yes ____ No ____

11 Do widely different ideas exist as to cause, effect, or indicated course of action?   Yes ____ No ____

12 Do expressed "facts" really have a major judgmental component?   Yes ____ No ____

Group Problem Solving as a Change Strategy Often it is the group as a whole—project group, department, or team formed for a special purpose—that is the target for change. The significance of group support and pressures in bringing about *individual* change has been noted at various points, and the above discussion in connection with conflict management suggests that group processes constitute a potent force for dealing with *common* needs and issues.

In addition to the gains from pooled rather than single efforts to identify better ways to handle things, broadening the base of people exposed to "solving" a change situation also increases commitment to the change. Group problem solving involves a nominal set of steps,* some of which correspond to those set forth for managing or resolving conflict:

1 *Define the problem so as to assure clear understanding by those involved.* Teams and ideas have different meanings for different people. Ask people to provide feedback in their own words to ensure that everybody is looking at same matter.

2 *Set the climate and procedures for problem solution.* Members need to sense the desire of the group leader for cooperation and interaction.

3 *Develop alternatives.* These must reflect the contribution of all group members. Thus, each person should be given a chance to set forth his or her ideas before any general discussion. Also, there must be adequate identification and development of related information—alternatives can be no better than the adequacy of information underlying them.

4 *Identify retarding and supporting forces.* People, events, rules, policies, and the like can act to encourage or inhibit development of various alternatives. The relative impact of each of these factors should be identified.

5 *Agree on evaluation criteria for alternatives.* Identify the objective and qualitative considerations to be used in evaluating each alternative and the importance to be assigned to each. Also start to consider bases for implementation as these may influence choice.

---

* See Morris and Sashkin, *Organization Behavior in Action,* for more on this.

6 *Select from your alternatives and outline the plan for action.* Make sure that the group recognizes the change in focus of the discussion from *what to do* to *how to do it.*

7 *Develop an action plan for launching change.* This action plan should capitalize on the insights and contributions of group members. Activities, step-by-step movement, and timing are all part of this approach.

8 *Establish an evaluation procedure.* Determine *who* is to do *what, when,* and *how.*

When Is Change Really Change?

A common complaint against some aspects of training and development is that the effects do not last. Once a person returns to the same old problems and associates, it is difficult to maintain that wonderful new self. Or inability to change others may result in increased frustration. After a management seminar, the following typical comments were expressed:

"The presentations have been interesting and worthwhile. But how do I convince my boss that we have to do things differently?"

"In two days I'm back on the firing line and ready to go. I've got new techniques—you've gotten me worked up and I'm enthusiastic. But I'm going back to an organization where they don't know as yet that the seasons have changed and it's time to put on a different set of clothing."

The need for shared understanding and group support suggests that careful thought must be given not only to what but *who* is included when training is undertaken. Whom to include will become more obvious if it is recognized that (1) a common frame of reference is necessary for sustaining or implementing change following a training program, and (2) it is the training experience itself that creates this frame of reference.

Change Resulting from Training and Development Activities

If you have taken part in any form of nontechnical training and development, what sort of change did you experience in yourself?

Skills or ways of changing things

_____
_____
_____

New or improved relationships

_____
_____
_____

Other Barriers to Change

Often technical and procedural factors, rather than human relations problems, are obstacles to change. Sensitivity to human needs cannot alone change certain organizational realities such as poor equipment or badly designed installations. This, of course, does not eliminate the need for developing interpersonal skills. It does underscore, however, our previous remarks that it is necessary to be clear about goals before embarking on a training plan.

Technical Training

To learn new skills or to improve old ones is clearly to *change*. But some important side effects may be less noticeable. Although specific skills may increase your market value in measurable dollars-and-cents terms, subjective gains are difficult to assess. Self-respect is greatly boosted by feelings of competency and mastery, but it doesn't stop there. Greater regard for yourself means reassurance and security for *further* change.

Increasing Motivation and Performance

Good as all this sounds, people are not always motivated to acquire new skills (DO I WANT TO CHANGE?) either where training is a matter of personal choice or necessitated by a job or work rule. Sometimes, as discussed in Chapter 3, people are secretly fearful of their ability to carry through (DO I HAVE THE ABILITIES TO CHANGE?) or unable to foresee what training can mean for them (HOW DOES CHANGE AFFECT ME?).

Organizations have an important role to play in these and other matters associated with training. Members deserve to understand the need for training as it relates to company and departmental development (WHERE HAS CHANGE TAKEN PLACE?) and thus to personal destinies (HOW DOES CHANGE AFFECT ME?). Training must be visibly related to stated goals. It should also be conceived and carried out in a way that builds on, rather than undermines or ignores, past contributions or individual capabilities.

Training, as a stimulus or facilitator of change, requires individuals to drop or shift older skill patterns and demonstrate new activity patterns. It is assumed, at times in error, that these newer patterns can be performed efficiently once training is completed. But efficient performance in the newer job state depends on the multiple considerations mentioned so far—motivation of the trainee; sensitivity to the trainee's background; adequacy of the training; effectiveness of the trainee's supervisor as a model; support of work associates; and the appropriateness of the new skills for job performance. The criteria for training effectiveness must therefore be expanded to include management of the entire change process. Performance levels are just the end of the line!

Ideas for Improving Technical Training Program

If you have been involved in some technical training program, either as trainee or planner, was sufficient attention directed to:

- explaining company plans and problems? Yes ____ No ____
- the personal concerns of potential trainees? Yes ____ No ____
- training methods? Yes ____ No ____
- characteristics of instructors? Yes ____ No ____
- the applicability of training to job requirements? Yes ____ No ____

What are your recommendations for improving the next program?

_____
_____
_____
_____
_____

Time and Change

Helping others to change naturally suggests active intervention, and we have accordingly discussed various steps to take. It may sometimes be wiser, however, to promote change in a more passive manner by letting time do the work.

Time works its own magic. That is what we bank on when we tell someone to "sleep on it." Time allows things to settle down, sink in, cool off, or build up. It also leaves room for additional things to happen. All this leads to a new synthesis of the elements, and this is *change*. Over the longer haul, time can help to bring change—experiences accumulate and the shape of things or direction for action becomes clearer. Experience provides an ever different information base from which to evaluate the past and the present and to think about the future.

Time may succeed where attempts at direct influence fail. Most people know this, whether in avoiding an irritable boss who just lost out on a big transaction or comforting the grieved through the reminder that time heals. Such knowledge may not, however, play enough part in *planning* for change. Thought should be given to the types of situations and persons most likely or capable of changing, using time rather than direct pressure. In short, when there is faith in the ability of others to come around in *time* to a *changed* way of thinking, time in itself can be an effective change strategy.

Choosing Methods—Preliminary Steps

We have given more-or-less equal weight to the various measures for bringing about change discussed, but of course they are not equal. Nor is there unlimited choice. However, the options may be greater than you think.

Systems thinking is a necessary framework for a clear understanding of the whole change situation. It should precede any planning details. Systems thinking will help you to determine general needs, interrelationships, and possible side effects of change. It will help you to discover what *you* can do. Take account of:

- **The task**—What attitudes and activities must be accepted, learned, or developed to bring about the change? If, for example, the change involves retraining to use new equipment, employees must be helped to understand and accept the reason, to trust their ability to learn, as well as to actually learn the new skills. All of this leads to many subtasks.

- **The time span**—How much time is required? How much time is available? Using the example above, the time required for retraining would include the technical and psychological factors. The minimum time would have to take into account acceptable levels of performance and the time required for changing related attitudes, habits, and the like. Estimation of time needs also involves consideration of short run versus longer run effects of a new activity. The passage of time will contribute to the scope and depth of the change.

- **Persons Involved**—Which and how many persons are affected? Any plan must be adjusted to the number and ranks of those touched by the change and, as already pointed out, their readiness for the change. This means that point of entry should be geared to: WHERE HAS CHANGE TAKEN PLACE? HOW DOES CHANGE AFFECT ME? DO I HAVE THE ABILITIES TO CHANGE? DO I WANT TO CHANGE?

- **Relationship to the organization as a whole**—How widespread is the desired change? Does the retraining involve a few people, a department, or the entire organization? If more limited, what other parts of the organization need to be informed?

- **Degree of change required**—Is the change minimal or extensive? Does the retraining call for altogether different skills to operate the new equipment or a slight change of present patterns? Remember that an objective evaluation may not coincide with the perception or feelings of those who must do the learning.

- **Resistance**—Is the need for change more-or-less accepted or strongly resisted? Does retraining threaten the security of those involved or some other area of individual concern?

- **Organizational resources and constraints**—Is the climate right for innovation? How much does your organization encourage new approaches? Are they likely to support your ideas? Personnel: Is there a range of in-house expertise? Financial state: Can the firm afford to engage outside help, divert time from ongoing production, and so on? Relationship to the larger environment: Does competition or

Helping Others to Change

DIMENSIONS OF THE TASK

METHODS	The task itself	Time span	Persons involved	Degree of change required
Focus on Circumstances				
Hat changing				
Environment changing				
Messages				
Reward and punishment				
Focus on Persons				
Friendship, admiration, respect				
Training and development				
Technical training				
And Don't Forget:				
Time as a strategy				

continued

Helping Others to Change (continued)

RESOURCES AND CONSTRAINTS

Resistance*	Organizational resources and constraints†	Your resources and constraints‡

*Try to take account of where resistance originates: WHERE HAS CHANGE TAKEN PLACE? HOW DOES CHANGE AFFECT ME? DO I HAVE THE ABILITIES TO CHANGE? DO I WANT TO CHANGE?

†Include: climate for innovation; personnel; financial state; relationship to the larger environment

‡Include: formal authority; informal power; knowledge and skills

availability of human or physical resources change any of the above realities? For example, does a large local labor pool unduly influence the attitudes of management toward present personnel?

- **Your resources and constraints**—What is your formal authority? To what extent do you possess informal power—how much are you liked or respected? Finally, what knowledge and skills do you possess? What do you know that is especially relevant to the desired change? Have you, for instance, mastered the new skills yourself or been involved in similar retraining plans in the past?

The chart on pp. 110–11 brings together the previous described *change strategies* and the considerations outlined in this section. It will aid you in thinking through and selecting methods suitable to particular tasks.

Matching Methods with Need

Suppose that as a manager your immediate role in a retraining task involves informing those to be retrained about what is going to happen. Thus your initial job is one of preparing people for change. This calls for a communications approach that will: (1) announce to them that change is about to take place *and* that it will affect them; (2) build motivation to change; and (3) make it clear that they have the abilities needed to change (for retraining). Your choice of methods for communications will be affected by the various factors we have enumerated—time pressures, number of people to be retrained, and so on.

Facts of the Matter   Continuing with the present example, let us say that time is short for all aspects of the retraining task due to competition from other companies; that thirty people are actual candidates for retraining; that the new skills are not unduly difficult to learn, but that your past experience warns you to expect at least some resistance due to ignorance of the situation (WHERE HAS CHANGE TAKEN PLACE?); that your organization is not averse to trying novel ideas; and that although you do not know the training candidates personally, you do know they like and respect their immediate supervisor.

Selection of Methods   Turning to methods for bringing about change, which are listed in the left-hand column of the chart on p. 110, it is clear that some are more workable than others as ways to inform employees of the intended change (retraining). Those methods that seem especially pertinent to this task are: Messages; Reward and punishment; Friendship, admiration, and respect; Technical training.

Messages are more effective when the information for change can be conveyed or interpreted by trusted coworkers. Reward will help ensure that compliance is voluntary and cooperative. Friendship, admiration, and respect tap the power of work associates to exert influence on their members (especially where cohesive relations exist). Also, management can gain respect and thus the confidence of employees by playing a more visible and participatory role. Technical training will indicate expanding plans, beyond teaching necessary skills, to take account of the motivation and personal concerns of employees.

Gaining Acceptance   To encourage acceptance of the change, the employees' immediate supervisor should be consulted for advice and play a direct role in announcing the change. Since the target group is relatively small (thirty) and the firm appears open to new ideas, a day could be set aside for informal explanation by the manager *and* the supervisor. Having both appear demonstrates the importance of the retraining, the support of the organization, and the support of the work group's authority figure (its supervisor). An open and informal session would help to make visible the "real" reasons for the program, hidden fears, problems that might be encountered, and ways of dealing with them.

Another Application Example

Continuing with the same retraining example, suppose your responsibility as a manager is to help a training instructor plan the actual form and content of instruction. Reviewing each method we have discussed for promoting change would suggest some usable ideas. Concerning *technical training*, you would be alerted to the importance of making a credible case for *why* the training is necessary—a point taken account of in the first example. The why may be as important to the training instructor as to the workers! Managers often don't take on this type of responsibility, but more attention to such obvious needs could improve the chances for success when the program actually begins.

In the present example it is especially important that the actual training experience fit the explained goals and take account of each person's past work history and skills. As manager, you would be well-advised to make sure the instructor really comprehends his or her part of the mission, and has the personal traits as well as professional competence for carrying it through. It would be beneficial for the instructor to know each trainee's background with the company—a reasonable task for the number of people involved.

Both manager and instructor might find it helpful in planning the training to do some *hat changing* by assuming the role of trainees. This would enlarge their awareness of both physical and psychological blocks to learning. It would suggest improvements over armchair plans, which are often unrealistic because they are too far removed from actual needs.

How to Begin

To summarize, we have presented an approach for guiding change: (1) identify as fully as possible the dimensions of the task, the resources that may be brought to bear on it, and the prevailing constraints; (2) carefully review the change methods or principles described to determine which are most promising and feasible in light of the above.

The chart on pp. 110–11 should help you to follow through these steps. Choosing a workable plan is not easy, but in the process you will develop some solid ideas about *why* you are doing *what*. You can test out these ideas and learn from them, and that should yield real improvement over hit-and-miss approaches.

In Brief

Changing persons (rather than circumstances) or change as an outgrowth of influences that affect personal values and skills includes the following strategies:

Friendship admiration, respect	Basis on which to model beliefs and behavior
Nontechnical training and development	Improved interpersonal understanding and skills
Technical training	New skills and related gains in self-worth and confidence

The passage of time—allowing new forces to come into play—is yet another way to promote change.

Selection of a suitable change strategy becomes easier when preceded by clarification of the dimensions of the change task itself and the accompanying organizational and personal resources and constraints. A chart helps to simplify the whole process of matching change methods to change needs.

The next chapter looks at what the field of Organization Development can contribute to your ability to manage change.

Action Checklist

1   Can you count on confidence or trust to work for you in a change situation? Yes ____ No ____

continued

Action Checklist (continued)

2   Are there instances where your participation with other organization members might strengthen or improve the bases for change?   Yes ____   No ____

3   Can you distinguish individual development approaches from group development approaches as possible change strategies?   Yes ____   No ____

4   Do you understand how conflict management can lead to constructive change?   Yes ____   No ____

5   In encouraging or helping people to change, are you also considering the modification of environmental factors to increase the chances for success?   Yes ____   No ____

6   In viewing change needs and situations, are you able to distinguish between human and procedural or technical considerations and then establish the relative importance of each?   Yes ____   No ____

7   Do you take time itself into consideration as part of a change strategy?   Yes ____   No ____

8   Needs analysis seeks to identify needs and then match appropriate methods to these. Are you able to carry this out based on the model for "Helping Others to Change"?   Yes ____   No ____

Organization Development as an Aid to Change 8

In the U.S. there is considerable fascination with planning, and much attention is devoted to this phase.

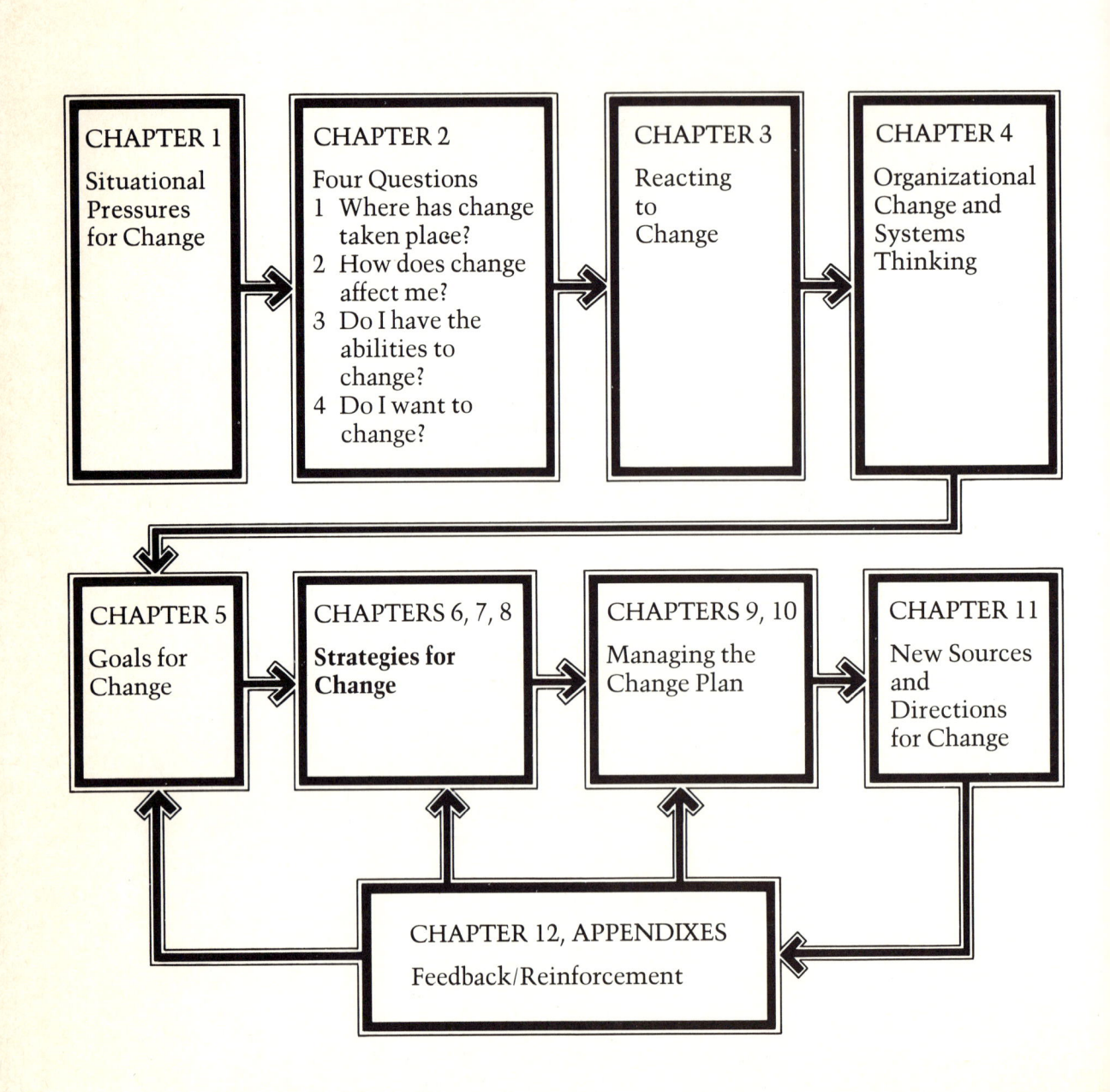

```
┌─────────────┐   ┌──────────────────┐   ┌─────────────┐   ┌─────────────┐
│ CHAPTER 1   │   │ CHAPTER 2        │   │ CHAPTER 3   │   │ CHAPTER 4   │
│             │   │                  │   │             │   │             │
│ Situational │→  │ Four Questions   │→  │ Reacting    │→  │ Organizational │
│ Pressures   │   │ 1 Where has      │   │ to          │   │ Change and  │
│ for Change  │   │   change taken   │   │ Change      │   │ Systems     │
│             │   │   place?         │   │             │   │ Thinking    │
│             │   │ 2 How does       │   │             │   │             │
│             │   │   change affect  │   │             │   │             │
│             │   │   me?            │   │             │   │             │
│             │   │ 3 Do I have the  │   │             │   │             │
│             │   │   abilities to   │   │             │   │             │
│             │   │   change?        │   │             │   │             │
│             │   │ 4 Do I want to   │   │             │   │             │
│             │   │   change?        │   │             │   │             │
└─────────────┘   └──────────────────┘   └─────────────┘   └─────────────┘
```

- **CHAPTER 5** — Goals for Change
- **CHAPTERS 6, 7, 8** — Strategies for Change
- **CHAPTERS 9, 10** — Managing the Change Plan
- **CHAPTER 11** — New Sources and Directions for Change

CHAPTER 12, APPENDIXES

Feedback/Reinforcement

One of the most important new sources of successful change programs has been the field of Organization Development, or OD, as it is usually called. This field has rapidly established itself and achieved considerable prominence among all types of organizations and practitioners. The present chapter is devoted to a discussion of OD principles, since we believe that: (1) managers should have some understanding of the OD approach to change if and when they are involved in organization-supported OD efforts; and (2) managers working on their own, or promoting change more-or-less independently of large scale organizational plans, can profit from OD thinking and experience.

What OD Is All About

Although we have approached change primarily from the manager's level and needs, there is general convergence between OD practices and the ideas set forth throughout this book. OD, however, takes a comprehensive and systematic approach to organizational success—whether it is measured directly in sales dollars or reflected in customer service or personnel performance. OD efforts may be applied at various levels such as departments, divisions, or an entire organization. But whatever the unit, emphasis is more likely to be on general diagnosis, planning, and building, rather than on troubleshooting in isolated areas. On the whole, OD personnel are not connected directly with the responsibilities and problems that managers face—they are in this sense *outsiders* who must gain knowledge of what is going on in all parts of an organization.

Organization Development Guidelines

Some OD propositions useful for our purposes include the following:

1 Changing activities and people requires dealing with both the climate surrounding work activities and the

people themselves. (This has been repeatedly stressed, particularly in Chapter 3 in discussing the reasons for resistance to change and in Chapter 6 where the distinction was drawn between changing people or their surrounding circumstances.)

2 People are dependent on other people and circumstances for success in their area of interest or assigned responsibility. Administrative activities and work functions are linked together in logical arrangements, so that it is rare that individual or circumstance can be isolated for change. (The significance of human support was discussed in Chapter 7 as a change strategy.)

3 Change programs start with the individual or with circumstances. Eventually change programs deal with both. The critical elements of a change program include:

- the individual,
- individuals and their immediate task group,
- work activity or procedure,
- group-to-group relationships and functions,
- environment or climate.

(This listing of change program elements is a consolidation of points brought out earlier concerning the need to take account of individual awareness and motivation for change, group ties, acquisition of appropriate skills and patterns, relationships to other parts of the system, and external conditions that facilitate desired change.)

4 Planning for change requires the establishment of priorities and time schedules. (The importance of clarifying goals and specifying reasonable subgoals was discussed in Chapter 5.)

5 Beyond implementation, change programs must include monitoring of results and redirection if indicated.

(This underscores the need for continuous reexamination of goals discussed in Chapter 5.)

6 Change processes extend over a considerable period of time. In some instances the adjustment of individuals or situations may require months or even years. Change effects may be comparatively isolated or touch greater numbers of organization areas than visualized initially. Thus, time scheduling, allowing for the redirection option may encompass a long period. (Systems effects are not always predictable in time or scope, but they should be anticipated and planned for, as we noted in Chapter 4.)

Don't Make a Big Deal Out of It

The above points may suggest that OD-directed change programs involve complex or highly detailed procedures. In truth, successful OD change takes conscious study but need not be overwhelming. What is important is to work out a plan that is complete and takes into account *goals, approach, appraisal of accomplishment,* and *redirection as needed.* In the United States there is considerable fascination with planning, and much attention is devoted to this phase. Unfortunately, effort then tends to fall off rapidly—and too often short of successful accomplishment—the result of insufficient follow-through.

How Long Does Change Take? There is no specific answer to this question, since change depends on a number of factors. However, one thing can be said with assurance. Organization members, even planners and specialists, usually underestimate how long change takes to work through organization procedures.

The more obvious factors affecting the length of time for implementing change reflect the *magnitude* of desired change and the *numbers* of people involved. Extended time intervals for change typically involve:

1 considerable numbers of people (multiple departments or whole divisions, for example),

2 large-scale changes or radical departures from previously existing methods of doing things,

3 system adjustments that touch related activities and thus move in ever-widening circles.

In the first case, the sheer number of people and units involved leads to longer time periods for accommodation to the new techniques or ways of doing things. Similarly, when individuals or departments must carry out new approaches quite removed from older or traditional approaches, learning time and psychological reorientation to newer organizational demands require time intervals often far beyond those of the actual change.

Where system changes are involved, system balance is affected in that shifts in one area often require corresponding adjustments elsewhere; many of these are unanticipated.

Unanticipated Effects   It is worth dwelling on these for a moment because system-related changes may greatly extend time needed for change *and* may evoke unanticipated problems to boot. Two examples will make these points clear:

An insurance company developed a health protection package designed to provide low cost coverage with a completely standardized package of client (insuree) information and conditions. The policies were to be directly and easily entered in the computerized information system. But it turned out that people didn't quite fit the highly standardized format. Information adjustments made by agents could not be accommodated in the computerized procedure. System adjustments to the original change (a standardized package) and retooling in this case took almost a year and a half.

A group of doctors formed a medical association providing a broad range of medical services. As the practice grew, it became necessary to establish an office manage-

ment function because of the volume and diversity of client information and records. The nature of the practice shifted as various specialties were added to provide a more complete service. This made significant demands on records, information, and third-party transactions. Changes occurred in medical delivery and services, but these were not anticipated and required modifications elsewhere in the system.

Psychological Acceptance

Individual adjustment to change is a complex phenomenon and more difficult to deal with than technical or procedural matters. Technical and procedural matters are quite specific and will often permit the application of simple logic or tests of completeness. Along with these systematic checks, time estimates can be made based on previous experiences. Thus, the total time for installing a new computer-based procedure (after the design of the activity) reflects specific time estimates for various phases.

Methods and systems people deal with technical and procedural situations in a fairly straightforward way, but it is well to realize that this aspect of change may range from weeks to a year or better depending on the considerations mentioned earlier. Yet this is often the easier part of change. It is the people side that presents complications.

People are creatures of habit. They seek to perpetuate the familiar since this provides mental comfort and is nonthreatening. Because this is so, people may fail to accept change, continue to fight change, or adjust in only slow deliberate fashion, long after a procedure is installed. Two examples illustrate this point.

A department store installed a new information system that involved the conversion of cash registers to information and transaction registers involving credit cards and inventory information as well as direct cash payment. In the older system, it had never been necessary to be concerned with various types of stock or inventory information. Most of the emphasis was placed on customer service and cash register or ticket transactions involving nominal information. Although all employees were trained in the new procedures for two days, miscoded information and serious mistakes went on for months after the conversion. The younger people with little experience, many of whom were part time, found the change relatively easy to make. More experienced employees who had to change deeply ingrained personal habits were quite unhappy with the new requirements and comprised the major source of errors. People in this more experienced group felt "it won't be long before we get rid of this mess and go back to the other system."

A steel facility carried out a change that involved the replacement of an old batch type, steel sheet operation. The new installation was a modern continuous mill. Periodically a study was made of the adjustment of the employees to the greatly modified work conditions. The results indicated that employee outlook reflected wide ranges of satisfaction and dissatisfaction with the change in the line. Almost five years passed before individuals fully accepted their modified work conditions and turned their attention elsewhere.

These case studies emphasize the *time dimensions of change.* Judging time requirements is indispensable to the success of any plan. The magnitude of change (size and/or numbers of people) is an important and initial consideration. However, time requirements may be extended greatly due to the human dimensions of change that must be dealt with—often after the procedural aspects of change are complete.

Practicality of OD Techniques

OD is not a panacea for all organizational problems; rather, it is helpful in situations involving group development and intergroup relationships. The success of any particular intervention is at least as much of a function of the desire for success among leaders as the technique per se. The degree of success may also be influenced by the power of various people participating in the OD program and their ability to bring things to the attention of senior people, acquire needed resources, or get other related groups or individuals to make appropriate adjustments. Again it can be seen that time is required to work things out, even if the solutions are found early and the surrounding conditions are optimal.

Universal Problems

Those in OD proceed from a broad understanding of all types of organizations. They recognize the underlying similarities in the challenges they face. Both the similarity of change issues encountered among widely different organizations and the application of change principles are illustrated in the following two cases. One involves hospitals and the managers and personnel concerned with *admittance activities* involving incoming patients, doctors, and internal medical and nursing staff. The other situation, that of a food industry, involves the *purchasing* function charged with procurement, inventory management, and allied responsibilities.

Hospital Admitting Function and Change

The admitting function has assumed new importance in hospitals. It is a central means for developing patient information, a key activity in public relations, a monitoring and control activity in utilization of hospital facilities, and an initial point for cost and billing procedures. In past years, clerks, typists, and nurses often supervised admitting. This setup proved quite adequate. With the types of changes just described, however, the level of required managerial skills has become greater and greater. Central change issues involving people include the following:

1 How do we increase the technical, administrative, and conceptual skills of admitting managers?

2 Where people are qualified, how can they be convinced to undertake self-development to meet the increased demands of their jobs?

3 How do we improve the skills of individuals who must increasingly work through the hospital system in a cooperative or coordinated way?

4 How do we establish and/or enlarge professionalism among admitting managers?

Purchasing Function and Change

The traditional practices of purchasing were often narrowly conceived so that people from many different areas of the organization (marketing, production, engineering) could qualify, based largely on experience or availability. The growing complexity of work systems, greater dependence on computers for information processing, increasingly intricate materials, new importance of customer service and inventory dollars, and required compliance with all manner of new legal regulations have all helped to enlarge the scope and stature of purchasing functions. New methods that involve statistics, other types of mathematical analysis, and areas of financial management know-how are among the many new purchasing skills. Little wonder then that a major national association of purchasing agents has declared professionalism as a major society objective and concern.

Change—the Underlying Need

In a recent executive seminar, participants were asked to list their major people-related problems. Professionalism, better use of human resources, and acceptance of change programs were the major problems that emerged (and which are similar to those noted for the hospital admitting situation). In the broader view, all involve change in that *professionalism implies a state of mind as well as particular abilities,* and a shift in individual outlook is needed. Better use of human resources means changes in organizational policies and consequent changes in personal experiences.

Both the hospital and purchasing situations lend themselves to change strategies using OD approaches. This is the subject of the next section.

Change: Admitting Function at Uptown Hospital

Uptown Hospital was a medium-sized general hospital founded almost forty years ago by a group of doctors in a large midwestern city. Numerous environmental changes transformed the admitting function from a mostly clerical function into a complex administrative operation seen by the administrator as one of the key support activities.

Ruth Burchick was admitting manager. She had served in this post for almost five years. Prior to her promotion, Burchick was night admitting supervisor. Before this she had worked as a floor supervisor in nursing. She had found the nursing pace too hectic, the demands great, and the rewards few. Additionally, she wished to try out her supervisory abilities under different conditions.

For the first few years the new work proved to be a welcome change and Burchick found it quite stimulating. Then, with the expansion of the hospital's system, the growing rash of legal suits, and the new emphasis on cost containment, her problems mounted rapidly. Hospital administration insisted on better bed utilization, incoming patient complaints grew regarding delays and poor handling, and various insurance carriers complained about the mistakes in reports. Burchick also had to wonder about the mistakes of which she was unaware, those that fell through the cracks and which might be important in cost saving (such as billing mistakes). In desperation she went to Bob Norman, the personnel manager. (At this point Ruth Burchick knew that change had occurred and that it had affected her. But her decision to seek help was still a personal rather than an organization-imposed action.)

Assessment at Another Level Bob Norman reviewed the situation with Burchick and then followed up with some analysis on his own. He visited various nursing supervisors and department heads, and he got clearance for some patient contacts. He also talked to the business manager and to the controller who generally supervised the admitting activity. Burchick and Norman had the active endorsement and support of the controller to propose a program that would be beneficial to Uptown Hospital. Having concluded that their central objective was to improve admitting's performance, Norman's assessment of the situation was that a systematic change program was needed to solidify department leadership under Burchick. He also concluded it was important to improve individual performance, strengthen procedures, and work out better relationships with other departments. (Here Norman was acting as an OD specialist—in the sense of *making recommendations after doing a comprehensive study of the admitting function*, from the top down as well as from the bottom up, and as one somewhat more removed from the situation than Burchick.)

A Program for Change Norman and Burchick agreed that their program would seek to develop six key activities that would address the issues of professionalism, better use of human resources (upgrading of skills), self-development, and cooperation with other units:

1 performance review for all department members and identification of skill deficiencies;

2 specification of individual skill training programs;

3 self-development for Burchick, with some course work in leadership techniques, computer systems, and readings involving health field changes;

4 departmental meetings in which Norman, Burchick, and a few outside people would review health field changes, new developments at Uptown, current responsibilities and ideas for improving systems, relationships, and performance;

5 department head meetings at which Norman and Burchick joined other department heads to review working relationships and communications in terms of individually perceived department needs;

6 follow-up meetings between admitting and other departmental personnel to bring about improved working relationships.

Evaluation After some discussion between Norman, Burchick, and the controller, it was agreed that several different measures would serve as signs of progress: trends in complaints and impressions of selected department heads, and a sampling of patients' reactions. After a records base was established, it was expected that more specific measures, such as bed utilization, lost time, and samples of processed work, might be used. (Note that the OD approach does not stop with methods to bring about change; taking stock of *results* is of equal importance.)

Time Estimates Last but not least, in keeping with OD procedure, Norman felt it critical that a specific time frame be established for the activities that had been agreed to. This master time schedule was to be presented to the hospital administrator for approval and additional discussion where other department heads or hospital personnel were involved. Developing the time schedule proved to be a challenging task since it involved many uncertainties. No up-to-date information existed regarding the education, training background, and skills of department employees. Meetings were relatively easy to program; on the other hand, rates of individual learning would differ and thus require "best" estimates for time requirements. The plan finally approved covered a fifteen month period.

Results at Uptown Hospital Elements of the change program didn't go quite according to plan. This illustrates the OD principle that systems effects—both in time and scope—are never altogether predictable.

The greatest difficulties involved working relationships and resolution of problems with other departments. At times it appeared in the departmental liaison meetings that more time was spent attempting to decide what (and who) was the problem than was spent on the solutions themselves. Differing viewpoints on what constituted a particular department's responsibilities had at its base a failure to update procedures hospitalwide—changes had been undertaken mostly on emergency or problem bases and lacked an overall, integrated design.

The change program for the admitting department was relatively successful, however, in that Ruth Burchick was able to assert more knowledgeable leadership in her unit. Problems with patients were reduced, and quality of information improved. Most results were obtained with the medical and nursing staff. Better working relationships emerged in several key areas, but clearly more time would be required than originally estimated. In the end, the program took some twenty months rather than the initial estimate of fifteen months.

Change: Purchasing at Hilton Foods

Hilton Foods, founded in 1950 by Chuck Burton, achieved a national reputation in frozen foods over a ten-year period. From sales of under a half million dollars the first year, the figure rose to $12 million by 1960, and a national marketing organization was established and grew. By 1970, sales were almost $30 million and Hilton's lines included a variety of foods prepared in a production facility of advanced design and inventoried in a large automated warehouse.

At first, the purchasing function was run informally, with Chuck Burton making the key decisions and authorizing various purchases by the purchasing agent. As the business grew, Burton's time was taken up with other matters, and the purchasing agent was forced to make an increasing number of decisions by himself. As the volume of purchasing activity grew, two buyers were added to the office; one of the buyers was a production foreman from the shop, and the other, who had industrial experience, was hired from the outside.

In the early 1970s, it became clear to Burton that the purchasing activity had grown beyond the capacity of his purchasing agent. For more than a year, Burton and the agent had been having a growing number of discussions regarding the "fall downs" of purchasing in late deliveries, prices, off-specification product, inventory levels, mistakes in information supplied to the computer, not keeping records up to date, and so on. Finally, it was agreed that Burton would attempt to hire a person with more background and training in modern acquisition and inventory techniques. Alan Jay was hired as director of purchasing after an extensive search. He was a well-qualified person with twelve years of experience, a degree in industrial management, and graduate work in purchasing and inventory management.

From the very beginning Jay's time was taken up with a series of crises involving purchasing, inventory, and administrative matters, and he had little choice but to respond to the problems. After a period of almost three years, procedural and technical problems were coming up much less frequently and Jay decided to turn his attention to strengthening managerial and administrative performance. In his judgment, it seemed that what was lacking was: (1) good internal organization with purchasing department members working together effectively; (2) a better understanding of the purchasing function at Hilton Foods, its relation to production and inventory performance, and other factors influencing how well purchasing performed; (3) improvement of individual performance of department members, which appeared to be a mixed bag of motivation and skills.

An outside expert would be in a better position, however, to gather pertinent overall information on Hilton Foods and to make a diagnosis of the purchasing function—taking the entire organization into account—and to recommend a specific program to bring about needed change. With the support of the company president, Alan Jay worked out consulting arrangements with Dr. Michael Stein, one of his former university professors, who was a specialist in OD.

Application of OD Skills Stein visited all of the purchasing department members and also talked with key people in production, industrial engineering, product research, and several of Hilton's major suppliers. In a short time he had an understanding of internal flows of information and products and the relation of these to suppliers and external factors (such as prices and commodity markets). Stein was also able to size up the nature of personnel problems that affected bottom-line performance. It seemed clear that this performance could be significantly improved through better decisions that directly affected costs and indirectly (but with similar results) through the reduction of mistakes, turnover, and greater commitment to company performance. If purchasing was to benefit from these possibilities, then it would have to function as an organized team, sharing common purposes and working in a coordinated way.

Building Skills and Motivation The first phase of the change program concerned improving individual skills. It was critical that all department members have adequate skills to meet their work responsibilities before any team building began. Skill development ran afoul of a number of human problems. Some people were unwilling to admit lack of skills. Others felt they did not have the time. "That's for the younger people—I served my apprenticeship," was another response, along with expressions of fear and outright hostility. A variety of means were used to motivate people to undertake training. To begin with, training was approached as a highly individualized matter. Programs were tailored to personal needs. The cooperation of some of the stubborn but experienced members was secured by enlisting their help to provide background information on the company and its internal operations and relationships. Often important things are not officially recorded, and the knowledge of these experienced people proved to be very valuable.

A second avenue involved the use of hard evidence, such as records of late deliveries, complaints, and "outs" in critical items, to demonstrate the type and magnitude of some of the problems and to encourage discussion of them.

Finally, the developmental effort itself contributed to increasing motivation for improving skills. It conveyed to department members a concern for their problems. It also made clear that management was not out to take away jobs but rather to improve job performance.

Team Building   These approaches set the stage for the formal team building efforts that followed. First, a biweekly department meeting was regularly scheduled to provide the opportunity to air problems. Next, several off-site meetings were held as "planning and problem-solving sessions." Outside resource people were brought in to help guide the sessions and to help in development of workable solutions for the problems discussed. In these off-site sessions, department members were taught a planning and problem-solving procedure:

1   Establish *what* has to be done.

2   Provide the reasons *why* it should be done.

3   Determine *when* it will be done (timing).

4   Determine *who* will do it.

5   Establish *where* it is to be done.

6   Determine *how* it is to be done.

Small groups at these off-site workshops then worked on various problems and issues and brought them back to the main group. At all times, discussion was kept on a constructive plane with *positive reinforcement* for good ideas and suggestions for matters requiring further study.

Leadership   Alan Jay's departmental leadership was strengthened considerably by his role in the on-site and off-site meetings. The consultant, Dr. Stein, acted as a sounding board for ideas, but he made sure that department members looked to Jay and not himself for decisions or specific actions. In the course of the meetings, department members viewed aspects of Alan Jay's competency that were masked in the confusion of past years.

Systems Changes   At various points it became clear that a profitable purchasing operation depended on cooperation and information from other departments. As the development effort unfolded, a number of these critical interfaces were identified and purchasing performance improved through mutual understanding and/or procedural changes.

An Organization Development Experience

Organization development efforts, as a strategy for change, bring with them the promise of considerable benefits, but they are not without their costs in managerial and employee time. An OD effort may also involve the time and costs of an outside consultant to help get things started, to keep things moving, and at times to say and do the things that an inside person would find difficult or simply unwise. In addition, the manager considering the use of an OD approach must be able to demonstrate that it is a useful way to handle things and has a positive bottom-line impact. The person who is aware of the time/cost implications of OD and the power structure and intricacies of organization life can make good use of the OD model and where indicated involve an outside person (consultant) as a change agent.

The following illustration provides another example of a problem dealt with using OD ideas. The situation is a common one—two departments that must work together. Those interested in bottom-line results need think only of the wasteful, uncoordinated work and the time, energy, and monies used in argumentation or developing "evidence" to realize the necessity for some form of intervention. OD approaches have the potential for improving working relationships *between* departments while at the same time improving the way in which people relate to each other *within* units. These relationships are not merely social in nature; good relationships between department members can result in new ideas, improved solutions, and higher performance as the *joint product* of unit members.

Company Situation

A metal fabricating plant of G.F. Industries employed some 1,500 people and produced a line of industrial products for the transportation industry. Since many parts were fabricated to container specifications, production management and supervision were in constant contact with the engineering and quality control departments regarding specifications, quality problems, "deviations from print," customer samples, delivery problems, releases, and changes.

In the past two years, the pace and character of work had changed in the plant and in no small way was an initial cause of growing tension and occasional conflict between production and quality control. First, the addition of new equipment permitted the "selling of business," which was more complex than that handled previously. Second, some of the new equipment also provided much higher capacity. Consequently, the product mix started to shift as the sales engineers developed new business. Production and quality control had always been at odds with each other, reflecting the different roles each played, so that some conflict was expected. "If there's no problem, somebody's not doing his job" was the way John Nickels, the general manager, described things. But even the general manager wasn't prepared for the almost hourly battles that started to blossom as the new work was processed. Since production and quality control seemed unable to agree on anything and Nickels was running out of time (and patience) for coping with the situation, he called one of the managing associates of an industrial consulting firm that had undertaken some planning studies on behalf of the division in the past. The managing associate assigned a consultant, Marv Temples, to the project. Temples had OD experience plus a familiarity with plant problems and processes.

The OD Strategy for Change

Temple met with Nickels. After hearing the background of recent events involving production and quality control and interviewing the heads and senior people in the three plant departments (engineering, production, and quality control), Temple outlined his action plan to the general manager.

1   Outline of the consultant's role

- Act as a neutral party in the carrying out the OD process—a role and activity that is carefully explained to the departments involved.

- Keep departments/representative teams on track as the process is developed.

- Organize and conduct sessions.

- Guide the resolution of more deep-seated issues that are likely to arise.

2   Need for clarification of issues and problem resolution
The procedures of OD are not likely to bring useful results unless there is recognition by the departments or groups involved that a problem actually exists and that the matter may be resolved in a way that can be of value to each group as well as the company. Communicating this reality is an activity that takes place before any joint meetings of the departments involved. That there is a problem is usually obvious, but in some situations "proof" may have to be introduced, such as customer complaint records, turnover

trends, or budgetary figures. The fact that the matter can be resolved is sometimes an article of faith by the parties involved, a function of the consultant's reputation, or perhaps the confidence of the senior manager.

3 Initial orientation

- Introduction by the general manager

- Easel talk

- Describe role of consultant as facilitator

- Present sketch of overall procedure (see sketch, p. 138)

- Explain underlying ideas of OD program

- Relate OD sketch to the reality of plant situation

- Indicate how OD procedure will result in an action study

- Make assignment for each group

Meeting lasts one and one-half to two hours.

Initial Study Assignment   The purpose of the initial assignment is to establish a positive climate for change. The emphasis is on assets, or the plus side of the ledger. Each group has approximately one week to think about what the other group has been doing to help them in their work activities. When the groups come together at the next session these points are developed.

Work Session I (the "Positives")   Both the quality control and production departments had teams designated that represented the interests of each group. At the first work

Sketch of Organization Development Procedure, G.F. Industries, Metal Fabricating Division

- Recognition that problems exist
- Establish need for clarification of problems and issues
- Strengthen belief and need for positive actions that can benefit the departments involved and the organization, too

Initial Orientation Meeting
- purposes of program
- explanation of solution process and techniques
- bases for use of groups
- united homework assignment

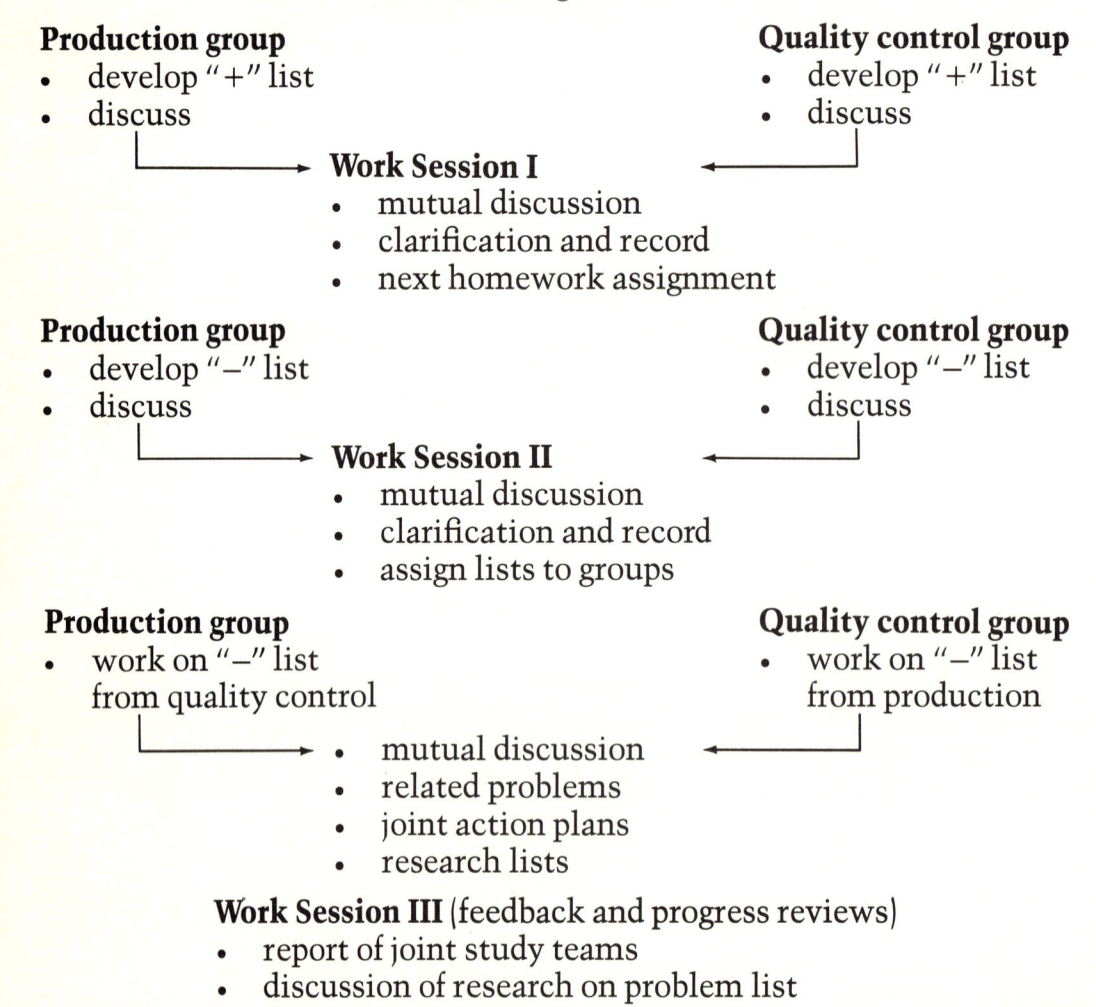

Production group
- develop "+" list
- discuss

Quality control group
- develop "+" list
- discuss

Work Session I
- mutual discussion
- clarification and record
- next homework assignment

Production group
- develop "−" list
- discuss

Quality control group
- develop "−" list
- discuss

Work Session II
- mutual discussion
- clarification and record
- assign lists to groups

Production group
- work on "−" list from quality control

Quality control group
- work on "−" list from production

- mutual discussion
- related problems
- joint action plans
- research lists

Work Session III (feedback and progress reviews)
- report of joint study teams
- discussion of research on problem list
- future action plans

session, each department's representatives met as a group and reviewed the positive ideas each had regarding the other department. Not surprisingly, this discussion started very slowly in both groups as people claimed that "we couldn't think of anything." The general manager attended this and subsequent sessions.

After a while, both groups were able to identify some items that were then presented to the group as a whole. Aside from starting things off on a positive basis, the group sessions also have the purpose of identifying other "forgotten" items, as well as activities and reports that may turn out to be no longer needed or of little value. At the same time, a group, upon learning the value of something it is doing, is encouraged to continue the procedure. Items were recorded on easel charts, then tacked on the wall for display at the next work session. Time for this session was about six hours.

Work Session II (the "Negatives" and Solutions) The next assignment each group received was to identify specifically what the other department was or wasn't doing to cause problems. Also, they were asked to think about the relative importance of these problems. The groups reconvened after one week. This time the session lasted for two days.

First, both groups met in private sessions to consolidate their lists and secure consensus on the relative importance of the problems. Second, the departments met in a joint session and each presented its negative list. The long awaited moment had arrived, but having presented the "positive" side first (and seeing these still tacked on the wall) took some of the sting out of the problem areas. Understandably, there were a number of times when arguments broke out, attempts to assign blame, promises to get the real facts, and the like. This session is a very difficult one because it leads into more deep-seated problems that the department people have often neglected. For example, in this situation, production talked about "technicians who went out of their way to find something wrong and reject an assembly" or "sloppy procedures—couldn't even get the same reading twice in a row from the same test."

For their part, quality control mentioned the production department head "who didn't seem to care about what the foreman and general foreman were doing—encouraging them to get the stuff out almost as if quality didn't count."

At the end of the first day of this work session, problems and priorities as seen by each group were recorded and tacked up on the walls. Problems that were technical in nature and that required records analysis, equipment checks, or more elaborate study were recorded for future investigation and resolution. Problems involving other departments, plant policy, and the like were also recorded for review by the general manager. The fact that Nickels sat in on these sessions assisted Temple in maintaining control and gave a graphic picture of some of the problems that had come up and even the part he had unintentionally played in failing to deal with these matters. Once the discussions got underway, nobody seemed reluctant to talk, even where the issue involved the general manager.

The second day of this session was devoted to problem solving but with each group assigned the problem list from the other department. Each was charged with developing an action plan and time schedule for dealing with the issue. These sessions lasted about half the day. In the afternoon, the groups from both departments met in a joint session for review of their action lists, developing *joint* action plans and *joint* study teams to research problem/solution approaches involving more deep-seated issues. Also, time targets were established for progress reports and feedback to all department members involved. Since there was a significant group of matters requiring four to six weeks for resolution, another session was scheduled to take place in six weeks.

Work Session III (Feedback and Progress Reviews) The production and quality control department teams, the general manager, and the consultant met six weeks after the completion of Session II. Not only were formal agenda items reported on, but department members were also asked to talk about the quality of work relationships. All agreed that both tension and conflict had lessened noticeably. Most agreed that they had seen some real signs of improvement and that at least an effort was being made to understand the other department's problems and work things out.

OD—Making the Effort

Various OD approaches represent a constructive way to deal with an important group of organizational problems. In the past, many of these went undetected or were ignored with the expressed hope that "things will work out." Unfortunately, deep-seated problems involving cooperation and working relationships often don't get solved unless there is a conscious effort made to solve them.

A basic aim in OD is to bring about *change,* and success depends on meeting the same conditions outlined in Chapter 2:

• Organization members must be *aware* of problems or opportunities for improvement that result from changing conditions.

• They must realize that the spinoffs from change *affect* them.

• They must know there are means (action programs, techniques, procedures) or that they have the *abilities* to bring about positive change.

• They must be *motivated* to change, able to anticipate the benefits from a course of action.

In Brief

Organization Development is an outside resource for bringing about change, whereas this book seeks to expand the individual organization member's personal resources for managing change. The insights and methods in either case are consistent; the language, emphasis, scope, and point of origin may differ. Typically, the OD approach is guided by extensive knowledge of all types of organizations, a systems orientation alert to delayed and unintended effects, and major concern with ultimate company performance. OD also goes beyond design and implementation to include systematic monitoring of change programs and necessary redirection.

The three case studies in this chapter illustrate the larger scale OD approach to change. They contain ideas and methods that have been elaborated in prior chapters. This should reinforce your confidence when it comes to independently initiating more ambitious change programs—as well as help you to work in comfortable collaboration with OD personnel.

Overall company policies are still another means for guiding change. Policy evaluation and how your own biases might contribute to policy are subjects covered in the next chapter.

Action Checklist

1 Have the reasons for OD efforts been sufficiently clarified? Yes ___ No ___

2 Has the responsibility for OD programming been clearly set out? Yes ___ No ___

3 Has a realistic time schedule been established? Yes ___ No ___

4 Do you understand that technical and procedural changes may lead people-related changes in the sense that adjustment to change may be slow or difficult? Yes ___ No ___

5 Has provision been made for monitoring, feedback, and evaluation? Yes ___ No ___

continued

Action Checklist (continued)

6 Have contingency procedures been considered for unanticipated problems?   Yes____   No____

7 Is the support of major officials visible to participants?   Yes____   No____

8 Is there "action research" competency to gather needed information on progress and problems?   Yes____   No____

9 Have the members of involved units been active in the OD procedure?   Yes____   No____

Policy Hang-ups that Can Block Change 9

Procedures concerning the selection of personnel reflect beliefs regarding the relationship of the individual to his work environment.

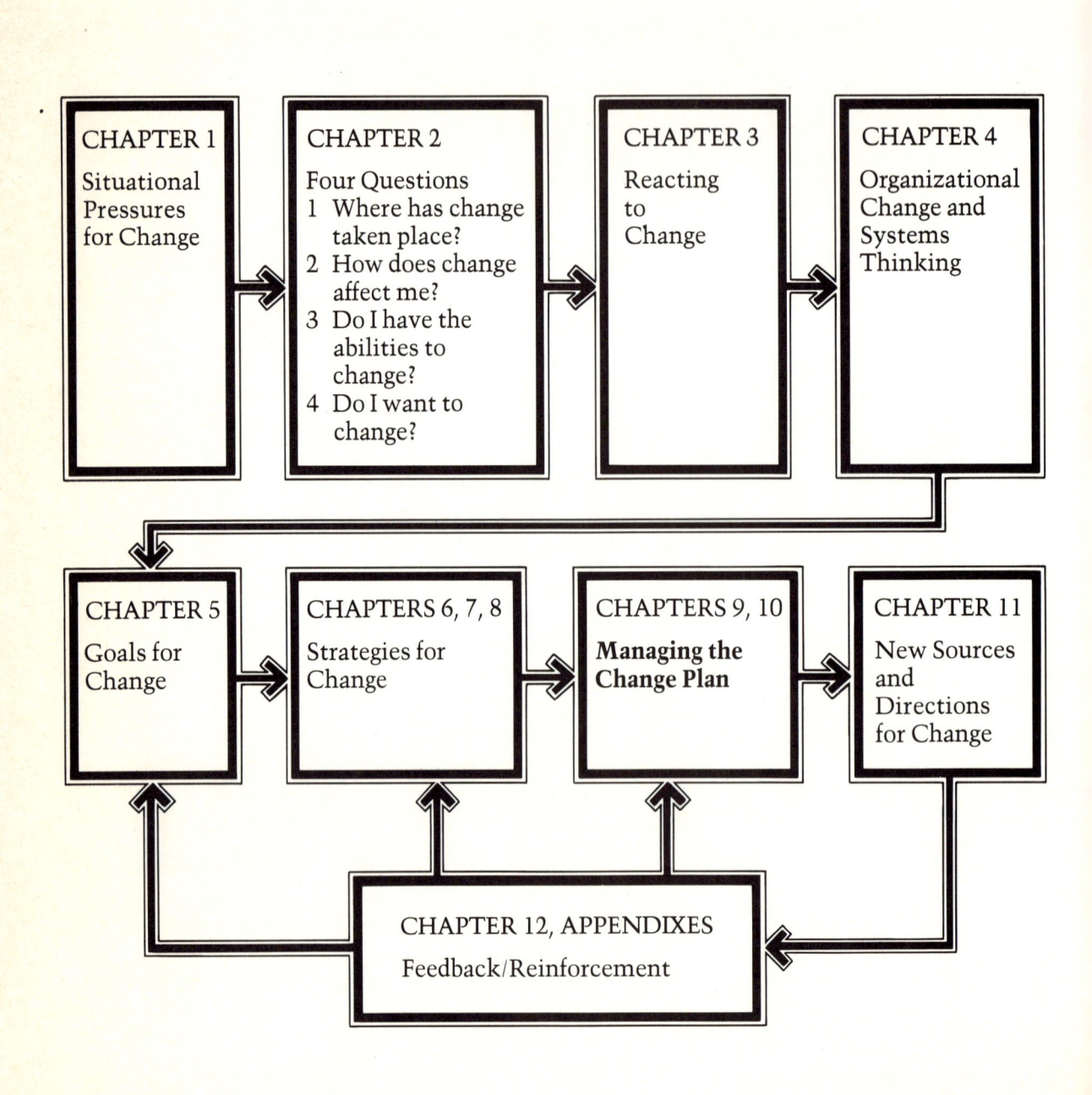

CHAPTER 1	CHAPTER 2	CHAPTER 3	CHAPTER 4
Situational Pressures for Change	Four Questions 1 Where has change taken place? 2 How does change affect me? 3 Do I have the abilities to change? 4 Do I want to change?	Reacting to Change	Organizational Change and Systems Thinking

CHAPTER 5	CHAPTERS 6, 7, 8	CHAPTERS 9, 10	CHAPTER 11
Goals for Change	Strategies for Change	**Managing the Change Plan**	New Sources and Directions for Change

CHAPTER 12, APPENDIXES

Feedback/Reinforcement

Organization policy is generally accepted as reality, the way things are. Individuals, however, make up organizations and therefore *create* as well as *respond* to policies. In the present chapter we examine some common personal biases bearing on change and how they may be reflected in organization policy.

Content and Validity of Beliefs

A bias need not have negative consequences. But it often represents a preconceived or unscrutinized belief rather than a carefully weighed preference. Some of these beliefs have to do with the way we perceive human nature. All of us have our own convictions about what motivates others and the conditions that make for success or failure, satisfaction or discontent. Other biases revolve about management principles and how to run a company, get business, look out for the future, and so forth.

All these pet ideas influence our everyday approach to changing ourselves and others. But they become *policy* (although this may not always be spelled out or recognized as such) when collectively subscribed to by management. The effects of such beliefs, therefore, can be very substantial.

Throughout, we have argued for taking a hard look at personal assumptions that color situations related to change. Now we urge the same hard look at general policies or operating practices—either those you have contributed to or simply have to live with. Do they actually foster desired change or work at cross-purposes? Are some policies in effect organizational hang-ups?

Recruitment and Training

Procedures concerning the selection and training of personnel inevitably reflect a set of beliefs regarding talent, the meaning of work to an individual, and the relationship of the individual to his or her social environment (including work). The following examples illustrate some of the ways these beliefs find expression in policy and what they may fail to take into account.

Monroe Insurance, a large underwriting agency, clearly subscribes to the belief that "good people will rise to the top." The underlying assumption is that some people are more naturally equipped than others to reach the top. Offhand, this seems harmless enough. Yet if competence is viewed as something that is present or lacking all along, the organization lets itself off the hook in several respects.

That is exactly what Monroe has done. It does not concern itself with discovering talent that is less than obvious. Nor does this organization provide any form of development opportunities—such as in-service training or subsidized college courses. As one official put it, "If our people want to improve themselves, they will find a way."

Monroe does pride itself on its selection procedures. These are highly standardized because "We know who and what we want." The company believes its methods to be both efficient and fair for meeting its needs. This emphasis on specific types for specific job slots is associated with a parallel tendency (which works against change) to keep employees in the dark regarding more general operations of the company.

Overlooking Potential Overly rigid criteria, along with standardized tests and interviews, may work against the best interests of the company. Such is the case if these measures fail to bring attention to certain types of personalities, talents, and backgrounds that may also have potential for contributing to organizational success. Outgoing people may make good insurance salesmen, but some shy people may work more effectively with certain types of clients; a secretary with slightly below par typing speed may turn out neater letters with no errors in spelling or have good ideas about how to run an office. An organization geared to the need for change may especially profit from incorporating different combinations and even different types of human resources.

Misfits and Breakthroughs Certain forms of "deviance" or wave making can be valuable. The person who sees things in a really different way is not always just a troublesome character who should be steered out or away from the organization. History makes it clear that we are indebted to many seeming misfits for important new insights, discoveries, or breakthroughs. Although there may not be many genuises who go undiscovered, organizations cannot afford to close their doors to less dramatic possibilities for innovation (desirable *change*). Overstandardization of selection *procedures* and/or *types* of personnel may eliminate creative new mixes.

Round Pegs and Square Holes

What is your own experience on this subject? Have you known some talented persons who failed to make it through an organization's screening process?

In your opinion, what might they have contributed to the organization?

	Rejected person	Potential contribution
Wasted talent	_____	_____
	_____	_____
	_____	_____
	_____	_____
	_____	_____

Are you yourself biased in favor of more "standard" types?

Living Up to Employees' Expectations

Recruitment and selection policies may keep many potentially valuable people out of an organization. Other practices keep people from remaining once they are in. A chief factor is failure on the part of the organization to meet employee expectations. Such expectations may originate with an individual's personal evaluation of an organization prior to accepting a job. Or they may be based on future rewards spelled out by the organization as incentives to accept employment. In either case, unfulfilled expectations are an important cause of turnover—which costs money and depletes the human resources an organization has chosen to invest in.

Organizations stand to gain by examining the connections between the possibilities they set forth at the hiring point and their policies for helping employees achieve these in day-to-day reality. Are the claims of the organization sincere? Are they realistic? If so, what tangible actions contribute to fulfilling them?

Living Up to Management's Expectations

To a great extent, we all strive to measure up to the expectations that others have for us. Therefore, when we are defined as worthy of succeeding, the chances are far greater that we will. When the definition is less flattering, we unfortunately tend to believe and act on *that*.

In Chapter 7 the work group and superiors were pointed to as sources of standards that have either an encouraging or an inhibiting effect on change. Company policy does the same. Such policy is not expressed in terms of friendship or camaraderie, but respect for the individual and his or her capacity to make a positive contribution are reflected in a variety of organizational practices. Some are more subtle than others.

Undue emphasis on supervision and petty conceptions of accountability demonstrate a belief that people cannot be trusted to work on their own, that work, in fact, is something that most people are trying to avoid. This bias may be self fulfilling—people who are led to feel that they are "no good" will not be overly eager to reverse that decision. Respect, on the other hand, can produce remarkable consequences. It often brings forth a clear "Yes" to DO I WANT TO CHANGE?

Translating Respect into Policy At the policy level, respect is a function of the nature (or suitable absence) of rules and regulations. However, it goes beyond that to encompass the kinds of opportunities an organization makes available. A company that is willing to invest in tuition reimbursement, to allow for outside schooling on company time, to arrange for in-house educational programs, or to subsidize travel related to professional development is demonstrating a belief in the capacity of its members to grow or *change*. Furthermore, such policies recognize that individuals are more likely to improve themselves under conditions that are conducive to these ends. Swimming against the current is both difficult and risky; swimming with the current may take the individual *and* the organization far.

Helping Others Help Themselves Evaluate your own biases on this subject. On the whole, are you inclined to be suspicious or trusting of others?

How does this express itself in your relationships with others? Do you tend to set traps for people? Or do you back up your faith in them through generous attitudes or acts?

Expressions of Personal Bias

Cite an example or two from your work experience and identify your bias in each case (such as a belief that people will cheat when they can or a belief that people will do a thorough job when given full responsibility).

_____
_____
_____

Relate these observations about yourself to a specific change you have desired to bring about. Describe how you may have helped or hindered that change because of your attitude toward others.

_____
_____
_____
_____

The Case for Participation

Optimists—with respect to the essential goodness of people—have less difficulty in subscribing to policies that aim at bringing rank-and-file members of an organization into the decision-making process. Those who are inclined to distrust the motives of others understandably fear and resist efforts to share power.

The ability to support wider participation in administration is also dependent on other attitudes. These have to do with willingness to let go or let matters take their course because of a sincere belief that it is possible to do things in better ways. A bias against innovation—change itself—lurks beneath much resistance to letting others in to help run things. This bias should not be confused with reluctance to believe others are trustworthy, or with unwillingness to share the *prestige* of administrative status. The latter also operates as a bias if it is assumed that personal prestige is diluted by sharing one's power.

A common complaint against greater participation in administration is that democratic procedures are costly, time consuming, and inefficient. To the extent that these arguments are readily accepted rather than thought through or tested, they, too, are biases that work against bringing about needed change in an organization. The inefficiency argument is probably the most acceptable one put forth for limiting access to the inner workings of an organization. It is easier to live with than the other biases discussed and certainly easier to present to others.

Cost of a Bias

The following illustrates a need for change that was recognized by all except the business owner himself. His bias against sharing responsibility became expensive company policy.

Joe Tobin was president of a retail food products company. From a five-person operation in which Joe did the buying, selling, and often helped with the food prepara-

tion, the business grew and became an extremely successful one in a few years. As the needs of the company began to change, Tobin's attempts to cover all the bases created real problems, technical and otherwise, for company managers. Tobin wanted to continue to play a central role in all decisions. Having developed the business, he could not believe that others were knowledgeable enough about it to make any significant contributions. Finding themselves more in the position of passive caretakers than administrators, managers began to leave the company. Tobin lost some good people to his competitors, and those who stayed on were simply marking time.

In closing the doors to full participation in decision making, Joe lost more than managers. He also cut off the multiple inputs and talents his business increasingly required for effective response to changing external circumstances.

What Is Your Position on Participation?

How ready are you, or would you be (given the authority) to involve more members of your organization in important decisions? If you like the idea, why is this so? If you have some reservations, what are they? Indicate your positive feelings or possible reservations.

Reasons
for position
on participation

_____
_____
_____
_____
_____

Although fact and fancy are not easy to separate, do you by and large feel your reasons above are squarely faced, whether flattering or not? Are you biased in that you have prematurely jumped to certain conclusions?

Chapter 9

Beyond Participation to Self-Leadership

At times, officials are at a loss to explain the apathy of organization members who should, by virtue of their positions and backgrounds, be actively and enthusiastically engaged in their work. Yet motivation may actually rest with the officials themselves—in specific actions that create a particular work climate. A recent experience in a university provides a dramatic example of the importance of work climate and also presents the most extreme argument for participation—by illustrating what can be accomplished with only *nominal* leadership when other conditions are favorable.

After twenty-five rather uneventful years, the School of Business at Franklin University, a small private university, attracted the attention of the wealthy Harrington family, which had acquired new business interests in the area. The family saw the school as having an increasingly important role in providing the type of education necessary for enlightened business planning and leadership to serve their own and community interests.

The university administration and the dean and faculty of the School of Business were able to make an excellent case for the future productivity of the business school, given generous financial support, and the Harringtons accordingly committed themselves to providing this support. Before these arrangements were completed, it became clear that a suitable dean could not be found in time to replace the incumbent dean, who was nearing retirement age. In order to present the best possible picture of continuing leadership, to avoid jeopardizing the Harringtons' decision, the president of the university strongly prevailed on the business school faculty to accept as dean one of the rejected but immediately available candidates.

The new dean came on strong, mandating a series of procedural changes and attempting to bring about a number of hasty curriculum decisions. Lacking respect for the judgment of the dean, faculty members resisted his leadership. The associated chronic frustration also inter-

fered with the independent pursuit of their own interests. After some time, it was apparent that the dean had to be replaced, whatever the risk to the school's image.

In short order, a new and promising dean was appointed, but things didn't turn out much better than the first time. The new dean appeared incapable of translating warm speeches into meaningful action and programs. The School of Business, now heavily endowed by the Harrington family, was going nowhere despite its new resources. The faculty sought the removal of the dean and a temporary appointment was made for purely administrative purposes.

After this, all kinds of positive changes started to take place. The initiative and creativity of individual faculty members came to the front as the "irritants" in their work environment subsided. They were functioning at their best level in an essentially leaderless organization. Competence alone does not ensure full participation in a common enterprise; a positive environment is also required.

Planning Is Not a Dirty Word

Planning—as an ongoing way of life—is still resisted by many organizations. A typical bias is that planning belongs to the realm of *special* events. As one executive put it:

The only time these planning approaches are warranted is when a division is contemplating a new plant or some unusual manufacturing or product development. This is not the case at Appliance Products. Our business has been quite stable for a number of years, and we have enjoyed a continuing steady sales increase.

The above comments also reveal a further set of assumptions—that planning is not called for as long as a business prospers, holds its own in the market, enjoys a good reputation for its products, and continues to stick to what it does. In other words, why rock the boat?

Why Plan?

The best reason for planning is that an organization that *systematically* attempts to look ahead can develop a set of alternatives with which to meet unforeseen or just dimly seen future eventualities *(changes)*. These may revolve about economic, technological, product, or people considerations—for example, a business recession, product changes indicated by development of a new material, or a shrinking labor market in a particular area. Last-minute decisions, without benefit of prior consideration, do not represent real choice. And to delay a decision at that point, pending further investigation, is often a luxury that a company cannot afford. A case in point is getting a new product into the market at the right time.

One company's experience helps to bring out the importance of a positive approach to change management.

Martin Drugs was a large retail drug chain with many neighborhood stores. For years it had been quite successful, but profits started to fall off as food chains moved into drugs. Martin Drugs then decided to change its sales strategy and approach. Its new program called for long-range planning on newer drug items likely to become popular and also sources of private label manufacture. It found that it couldn't compete with the food chains in local markets in the past because it didn't have the right product at the right price. Its new strategy paid great dividends as Martin was able to stock newer drug lines and also quickly identify sources of private label manufacture of conventional items in order to meet the competition's selling programs.

Peoplepower Planning

Too often, human resources are treated as expendable—as having a limited period of usefulness. This hidden bias accounts for failure to plan for future knowledge and technology and to prepare for personnel to acquire such knowledge and related skills. Obsolescence is *expensive*. It affects performance, turnover, morale, and the future state of any organization. No matter how loyal, industrious, experienced, or potentially creative, an individual who is lacking up-to-date knowledge or skills cannot contribute effectively to present or future organizational needs.

Organizations whose policy it is to counteract obsolescence through in-service educational and training opportunities and/or support of related outside activities have the edge on change in two ways: (1) they help to cultivate their own sources of change, and (2) they help to ensure that change has grass-roots support. This makes change more predictable.

Such organizations also protect themselves in another way. If the future productivity of women or minorities is not planned for as a matter of policy, this may limit promotional prospects—and usher in legal complications for the organization.

It is obvious that obsolescence may refer to any age, but where older people are concerned they are likely to suffer from a special bias. This is often self-imposed, but we refer here to the organization-imposed version—that people may be too old or set in their ways to change. Planning would help to avoid this congealed state. It should also be borne in mind that older personnel, like their younger counterparts, may also have *positive* reasons for supporting change and be just as adept at learning new things. Everyone deserves the benefit of the doubt.

Antichange Policy

Two more types of beliefs are worth mentioning since they add up to what might be called antichange policy.

Often, officials sincerely believe their organizations are insulated from change. "It can't happen here." This confidence, which may rest on superior or unique products or service, long experience in a field, or a captive market, may be well founded. On the other hand, overconfidence can be disastrous if it prevents contemplating the eventual effects of social, economic, or technical change.

At other times, the need for change is perceived clearly enough, but individuals feel that their organizations don't have the capacity to deal with it. They tend therefore to use their influence to discount the need itself (perhaps even convincing themselves) or to argue against change on grounds that it cannot be managed. The latter judgments are often biased in that they may be insufficiently informed regarding change principles, processes, and strategies—what it takes to create change. Although the change task may be genuinely difficult and beyond the resources of an organization, such a conclusion (and resulting policy) should rest on more than unknowledgeable impressions.

Does Your Organization Support Change?

The following items will help you to become more cognizant of company policy and to locate sources of bias in particular areas.

Recruitment: What kinds of people does the organization want to attract? Whose judgment is involved?

Are recruitment efforts:
- ☐ fairly local?
- ☐ broad in scope?
☐ Is the hiring process chiefly carried out by Personnel?
☐ Or is weight given to the judgments of key people in the appropriate department?

Is there evidence of a special "set" in hiring practices with respect to:
- ☐ age?
- ☐ sex?
- ☐ educational background?
- ☐ work experience?
- ☐ other?

Rules and regulations: What do these really communicate?

☐ Are rules and regulations minimal, leaving as much as possible to the discretion of the individual?
☐ Or is there a tendency to impose excessive restrictions in areas that are not of primary importance?

continued

Does Your Organization Support Change? (continued)

Professional development: How much does the organization value its members?

Does the organization provide:
- ☐ in-service training?
- ☐ tuition reimbursement?
- ☐ pay expenses for attendance at professional meetings?

☐ Does the organization actively encourage participation in the above activities?
☐ Does it *tangibly* reward such participation?
☐ Is a deliberate effort made at time of hiring to spell out organizational plans and what the employee can correspondingly expect in the way of personal advancement?
☐ Are training activities carefully matched with job requirements and opportunities?

Participation: How open is the organization to new ideas?

☐ Do work arrangements and organizational structure allow for sharing in decision-making?
☐ If so, is this process systematically employed?
☐ Are general suggestions or contributions of organization members *actively* solicited?
☐ Is there evidence that such suggestions are incorporated?

Planning: Is change conceived as event or process?

☐ Is it more characteristic to defer planning until special problems create a need?
☐ Or is planning engaged in as a routine activity?

Change itself: What is the basic position?

Is there a prevailing attitude that:
- ☐ change is good?
- ☐ change is bad?
- ☐ change is not called for?
- ☐ the resources for change are lacking?

continued

Does Your Organization Support Change? (continued)

On the basis of your responses what recommendations do you have for modifying policies to support change processes?

Policy recommendations _____
_____
_____
_____
_____
_____
_____

In Brief

In the final analysis, organizational policy boils down to the collectively shared beliefs of individuals. Some of the beliefs that find their way into the setting of policy rest on wishful thinking, half-truths, or simply uncritical acceptance of certain ideas.

Recruitment and training practices express convictions about what types of individuals best contribute to an organization, as well as how to go about selecting them. General respect for employees and their capacity for ongoing development (change) is demonstrated in policy ranging from everyday rules and regulations to that which makes provision for professional growth. Policy related to participation, inclusion or exclusion in decision making, reveals the extent to which an organization values the here-and-now judgment and creativity of its members. When it is policy to reserve planning for new undertakings only, organizational change may be impeded or less than satisfactorily managed. Policy that directly rules out organizational change may result from complacency or lack of knowledge regarding change implementation.

Unrecognized, the biases that enter organizational policy may sabotage its capacity for change. Those in a position to help mold policy therefore have an obligation to question their own beliefs.

In the next chapter you will plan a large-scale change effort, making use of what you now know about change: ways to *think* about it and strategies for *action*.

Action Checklist

1 Are significant changes affecting your unit or organization reflected in recruiting and selection approaches?   Yes ___ No ___

2 Are there concrete activities that demonstrate a belief in the capacity of organization members to grow and change?   Yes ___ No ___

3 Do some actions *discourage* individual initiative and positive identification with the organization?   Yes ___ No ___

4 Are you clear on your own position regarding participative approaches?   Yes ___ No ___

5 Can you incorporate planning as a systematic treatment of future eventualities and the identification of alternatives?   Yes ___ No ___

6 Is human resource planning (which integrates future organization requirements and personnel needs) an active organization approach to building change competency?   Yes ___ No ___

7 Do means exist for stimulating frank discussion of beliefs and assumptions that guide the making of policy?   Yes ___ No ___

Taking on Large-Scale Change 10

This chapter is concerned with the deliberate introduction of change throughout an organization.

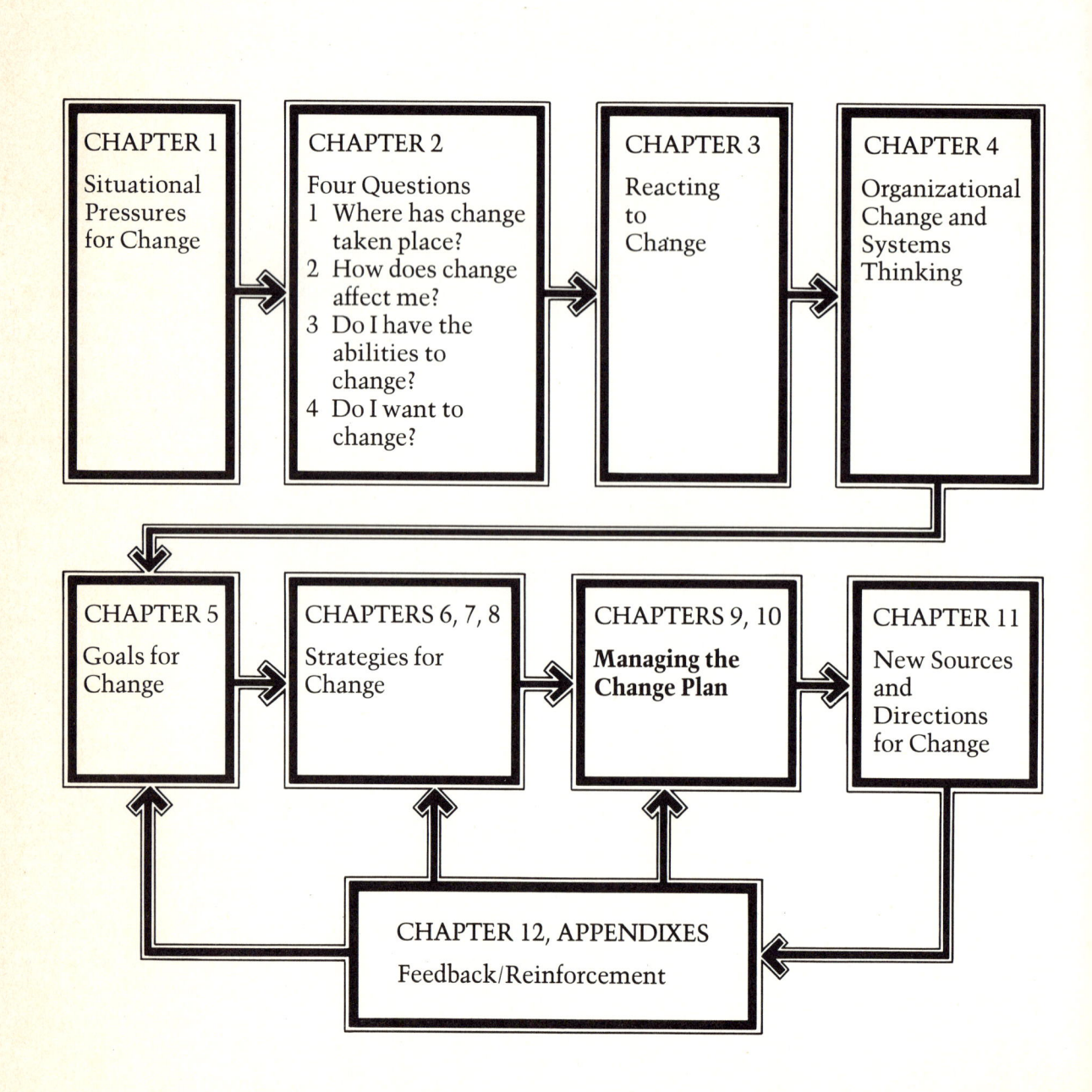

CHAPTER 1	CHAPTER 2	CHAPTER 3	CHAPTER 4
Situational Pressures for Change	Four Questions 1 Where has change taken place? 2 How does change affect me? 3 Do I have the abilities to change? 4 Do I want to change?	Reacting to Change	Organizational Change and Systems Thinking

CHAPTER 5	CHAPTERS 6, 7, 8	CHAPTERS 9, 10	CHAPTER 11
Goals for Change	Strategies for Change	**Managing the Change Plan**	New Sources and Directions for Change

CHAPTER 12, APPENDIXES

Feedback/Reinforcement

This chapter is concerned with the deliberate introduction of change throughout an organization. The purpose is to review your knowledge of change, apply it at a total system level, and then evaluate your skills for such an effort.

The need for change and the type of change are treated here as a foregone conclusion. Top management, perhaps in response to pressures originating outside the organization, may be responsible for such a decision, and we are going to assume that you have been assigned chief responsibility for carrying it out. In this capacity, your involvement with change will be less "personal" than in the exercises we have asked you to participate in all along—where stress was placed on bringing about change more closely associated with your own development or that of your department.

First, we shall discuss an instance requiring widespread organizational change, concentrating on the role of the executive in charge. Following this, you are asked to take on this role in an example of your own.

Guiding Extensive Change for Madison Plastics

Madison Plastics manufactures a quality line of plastic toys. The owners, Joe Mathews and Ben Charleston, anticipated new legislation setting forth more stringent safety standards that would place them at a competitive disadvantage. Recently they decided to take the bull by the horns and convert to more modern plastic materials and processes that would result in fire-retardant, stronger, non-toxic toys. The decision called for design modifications, some new equipment, and retraining in manufacturing techniques. It would also affect the other departments that comprised the business: office functions, personnel, purchasing, shipping, promotion, and sales.

It was agreed that Charleston, who usually supervised internal operations, would be the one to orchestrate the change, which would involve about 200 employees. He was familiar enough with the overall procedures in each department, yet he relied on department heads to run things, with minimal interference from himself or Mathews, who handled promotion and sales and spent much of the time traveling.

Recognizing that this change called for careful thought prior to any action, Charleston's first task was to clarify his own position vis-à-vis others. Strong guidance on his part was clearly necessary since the whole company was involved. Yet he did not wish to jeopardize the goodwill or to undermine the authority of department heads. Furthermore, he genuinely needed their help. He decided to place himself, as much as possible, in the position of an "objective" outsider—to present the change task to department heads (who at an earlier date had played some part in the company decision), to gather their opinions and recommendations, and then to let these managers assume major responsibilities for a large share of the preparations necessary for launching the change. Charleston would plan and coordinate from the perspective of the *total* system, mindful of how interlocking activities were affecting goal achievement.

Measurement of goal achievement raised some questions. Product modification could be measured in absolute terms, such as training man-hours to effect the actual product change, equipment conversion costs, promotion expenses, and the like. More difficult to calculate was loss of time, competency, and work commitment due to employees' psychological insecurity in the face of change or similar problems flowing from poor training methods.

Thus, whereas policy (the change itself) had been clearly formulated, there remained a need to specify corollary or related objectives such as maintaining employee morale, developing maximum skill levels, and preserving existing leadership structures, as already mentioned. Once identified, these objectives contributed to the planning process, helping to suggest important activities and to order priorities.

Shape of the Task

Following are the general steps that emerged as Ben Charleston considered overall needs. Some of the associated questions, problems, and activities are also noted. The comments in parentheses relate each step to discussions in previous chapters.

- **Primary communication to department heads**—to inform them of the decision and to secure recommendations on procedural and human factors, including special problem areas to be taken into account.

    - This step helps to identify related objectives such as those mentioned above.

(Communication of this type supports the OD propositions that success is linked to recognition of dependence on others and that change requires dealing both with individuals and with the circumstances surrounding work activities. See Chapter 8. Soliciting the recommendations of department heads also conveys respect for their opinions, thus establishing a climate conducive to cooperation and identification with the change project. See Chapters 6 and 7.)

- **Development of actual technical and procedural plans**—specification of *what* and *how* things are to be done, including *alternative* means, where possible.

    - With outside consultation. This will be necessary for design and manufacturing that require advanced technological information.

    - Within and between departments. Planning will begin with manufacturing, but other departments should be represented in order to learn how they will be affected and to work out suitable accommodations.

(Building on information gathered in the first step—communication to department heads—systems thinking can then be used to determine the scope and types of activities that will be affected by change and must therefore be included in planning efforts. See Chapter 4.)

- **Development of training methods with pertinent department heads.**

    - Exploring the best learning techniques for developing needed skills will require outside consultation for manufacturing.

    - In all cases the suggestions of employees should be enlisted.

(Acceptance of the need for training and effectiveness of the training will be determined by sensitivity to the individual backgrounds of the trainees, adequacy of the instructors and methods, and relevance of the training to new activities. See Chapter 7.)

- **Formulation of a control system**—means for ensuring that things go right.

    - Establishment of a *master time schedule* for coordinating time requirements for support activities, such as designing and securing new packaging and announcement and promotion of improved merchandise.

    - Establishment of *subgoals,* such as levels of training or output to be achieved by certain dates. These goals should be realistic, yet the company has little experience from which to proceed. Best guesses will have to be obtained from both outside and inside sources.

- Establishment of *modes for communicating and resolving* inter-system and departmental needs, such as regularly scheduled meetings, distribution of statistics and other information related to progress, provision for in-house and outside consultation with experts. Two important truths are acknowledged here: (1) No amount of planning can eliminate all problems; (2) feedback is essential to constructive action.

(OD procedures are particularly geared to concrete results. Time schedules, priorities, and all activities that generate communication and feedback are basic elements in structuring change and checking progress. See Chapter 8.)

- **Communication of the change program to all personnel.**

    - Both means and content of communication should attempt to ensure employees' confidence in their jobs and the company, as well as understanding of change objectives.

(Some messages are more successful than others. See Chapter 6. Group solidarity and other sources of personal influence may also affect reactions to change. See Chapter 7.)

- **Preparation for individual change.**

  - This is a departmental function because it demands first-hand knowledge of personnel. Supervisors could profit, however, from a general discussion of why people might resist the change.

(Attitudes toward change are governed by many factors, often having little apparent connection with the change in question. See Chapter 3. The four question change model helps to diagnose an individual's readiness for change. See Chapter 2.)

- **Launching the program.**

  - Initiating training and rehearsal of new procedures. This should not begin without sufficient preparation along all of the above lines.

  - Actual shift in production. Some flexibility should be built into the schedule to ensure quality production and guard against loss of consumer confidence.

(The OD approach recognizes that time required for adjustment to change is never entirely predictable, because individuals vary in terms of psychological adaptation and systems effects are uneven and often quite delayed. See Chapter 8.)

- **Redirection**, in both training and actual production stages, following feedback from the control system.

  - If alternatives are formulated at the outset of planning, adjustment can be more efficient. A standby plan would forestall major delays, for example, in the event instruction methods prove to be inadequate.

(Evaluation is treated as an ongoing, rather than final activity in OD planning for change. See Chapter 8.)

Additional Observations

Looking back through this agenda (which is meant to be suggestive rather than complete) it became obvious to Charleston that a successful transition was dependent on the knowledge and leadership of his managers. With an appreciation for this, it was easy for him to approach his responsibilities as an adviser and coordinator rather than as a heavy-handed administrator.

Listing the elements to be tackled also helped Charleston to consolidate the knowledge he was capable of contributing at each point. This included "hard" data on the business as a whole and "soft" knowledge of human factors. Breaking down skills—like breaking down goals into subgoals—makes any task less overwhelming.

Planning Your Own Change Program

Put yourself in the position of a Ben Charleston. As a small-business owner or corporate executive, devise a plan for extensive organizational change. The only requirement is that you have sufficient familiarity with the organization to come up with a realistic task. We will help you sort out the requirements and evaluate your own abilities for managing large-scale change as you proceed. All that has been discussed to this point should enter your **thinking**. Here is a reminder of topics covered in earlier chapters:

1   The ability to see things from several points of view, **thus increasing understanding** of a situation demanding change.

continued

Planning Your Own Change Program (continued)

2 Recognition of and preparation for system effects stemming from change in any part of a system or organization.

3 Understanding the relationships between goal formulation and goal achievement (identifying related objectives; developing subgoals to make change more feasible and measurable).

4 Identification of underlying reasons for acceptance or rejection of change.

5 Determining weak links and points of intervention in promoting change.

>(WHERE HAS CHANGE TAKEN PLACE?
>HOW DOES CHANGE AFFECT ME?
>DO I HAVE THE ABILITIES TO CHANGE?
>DO I WANT TO CHANGE?)

6 Strategies for promoting change and the circumstances under which they are most workable.

7 OD as a scaled-up approach to change.

8 Personal bias as it affects organization policy; organization policy as it affects change.

Stating the Particulars of Your Example

As with Madison Plastics, assume the change is no longer an issue for debate. The decision has been made, and you are the chief person to carry it through.

Briefly state the nature of your large-scale organizational change:

_____
_____
_____
_____
_____

continued

Planning Your Own Change Program (continued)

Your Organization and You

Next, supply the following information:
1 Size of the organization: _____

2 How it is organized (departments): _____
_____
_____
_____
_____

3 Your (hypothetical) position prior to taking on the change assignment: _____
_____
_____

4 Why you were chosen to head up this effort (seniority, special know-how, excess baggage, whatever): _____
_____

The way in which you choose to answer the last question should reveal something to you about your general level of confidence.

Other Objectives Associated with the Change

What other objectives appear to be important as you think about the change to be introduced? (For Madison Plastics, there were such considerations as development of maximal skill levels using new equipment, filling of current orders, and promotion of new products.)
_____
_____
_____
_____
_____

continued

Planning Your Own Change Program (continued)

Steps Leading to Final Goal of Change Program

Considering these related objectives and the goal (change), what do you see as necessary steps in order to launch the process? Refer back to the Madison Plastics example for help in developing your own scheme.

_____
_____
_____
_____
_____
_____
_____
_____
_____
_____
_____
_____
_____
_____
_____
_____
_____
_____
_____
_____

Further Elaboration of Each Step in Change Process

Review each of the steps you just listed, providing additional details and comments regarding action to be taken. For example, what kinds of information might you require from a manager, what types of procedures need to be mod-

continued

Planning Your Own Change Program (continued)

ified, and what subgoals could be set up to monitor progress? The questions below (which focus on helping others to change and gaining the support of associates) may suggest points you have not fully considered.

_____
_____
_____
_____
_____
_____
_____
_____
_____
_____
_____
_____
_____
_____
_____
_____
_____
_____
_____
_____

How Are You Helping Organization Members to Prepare for and Accept Change?*

1 Have needs analyses been used to identify areas of improvement specific to individual rather than generalized requirements?　　　　　　　　　　　　　　　　　　Yes____　No____

continued

*Based in part on William G. Dyer, "What Makes Sense in Management Training?" *Management Review*, June 1978, pp. 50–56.

Planning Your Own Change Program (continued)

2 Has a training program oriented to these individual needs been worked out?   Yes ____ No ____

3 Has the opportunity been provided for people to talk out their feelings or "reality check" their commitment to the change program?   Yes ____ No ____

4 Are policies, procedures, and work arrangements being modified to fit in with the changed expectations or needs of those participating in the program?   Yes ____ No ____

5 Is time being given over to help individuals identify and cope with problems likely to arise in the course of change?   Yes ____ No ____

6 Will a capability be developed for modifying the change program if major unexpected needs arise?   Yes ____ No ____

Have Your Associates Made a Major Commitment to Change?

1 Are there individuals whose leadership is respected and/or accepted who are supporting the change program?   Yes ____ No ____

2 Do your associates understand the broader purposes of the program?   Yes ____ No ____

3 Do they understand how their participation can help to achieve objectives they personally value?   Yes ____ No ____

4 Is the need for change experienced as a significant pressure?   Yes ____ No ____

Where Do You Anticipate Problems in Your Master Plan?

Would one department head be ill-equipped to handle new responsibilities, for example? Could some adverse local publicity delay implementation? Do you think you could delegate considerable authority? What could you build in to offset anticipated problems?

continued

Taking on Large-Scale Change   177

Planning Your Own Change Program (continued)

Possible Problems	Possible Solutions
_____	_____
_____	_____
_____	_____
_____	_____
_____	_____
_____	_____
_____	_____
_____	_____
_____	_____
_____	_____
_____	_____
_____	_____
_____	_____
_____	_____

Evaluating Your Performance

How do you now judge your general aptitude for guiding large-scale change such as you have just outlined?

   POOR   FAIR   OK   GOOD

The following list will help you to analyze the various factors that feed in to your conclusion above:

	Source of strength	Source of weakness	Does not appear to be applicable
1 General knowledge of the organization	_____	_____	_____

continued

Planning Your Own Change Program (continued)

	Source of strength	Source of weakness	Does not appear to be applicable
2 Knowledge of other organizations	_____	_____	_____
3 Experience as a manager	_____	_____	_____
4 Experience in other capacities	_____	_____	_____
5 Technical competence in pertinent areas	_____	_____	_____
6 Professional contacts and/or information outside the organization	_____	_____	_____
7 General educational background	_____	_____	_____
8 Personality traits	_____	_____	_____
9 Confidence rooted in past achievements	_____	_____	_____
10 Ability to absorb and apply principles discussed in this book	_____	_____	_____
11 Other factors			

continued

Planning Your Own Change Program (continued)

Increasing Personal Skills for Change Management

Are the limitations that you note something you can change and, if so, how? For example, you may only slowly acquire more experience as a manager, but perhaps you can readily learn something more about your organization by reviewing the propositions in this book.

Limitation	Action

In Brief

Management of change on an organization-wide basis must encompass total system performance and the relationships among subsystems. This is a difference in scale of application rather than in basic principles associated with change at other levels.

All topics covered in previous chapters are applicable to the large-scale change program you were asked to propose and plan for in this chapter. Although it must inevitably oversimplify the requirements and dynamics of the change task, such an exercise helps to confront real needs, to consolidate experience and new learning, to chart a sound and practical course of action, to assess confidence, and to identify personal limitations that may be modified.

A recent and different type of challenge for individual change is described in the next chapter.

Action Checklist

1 In developing a change program that reflects a general organizational need, are you able to clearly state the goals?   Yes ____   No ____

2 Can you work out a detailed set of steps leading to these goals?   Yes ____   No ____

3 Do you understand what information is needed both to institute the program and monitor its progress?   Yes ____   No ____

4 Can you secure the understanding and involvement of those directly affected by the program?   Yes ____   No ____

5 Is there commitment of organization leadership, staff, and resources needed for successful task completion?   Yes ____   No ____

6 Are you able to foresee problems that are likely to arise and understand how these may be dealt with?   Yes ____   No ____

7 Do you have general confidence in your own abilities to carry out such a change program?   Yes ____   No ____

Credentialing of Professionals to Meet the Demands of Change

11

It is likely that credentialing with enter your life.

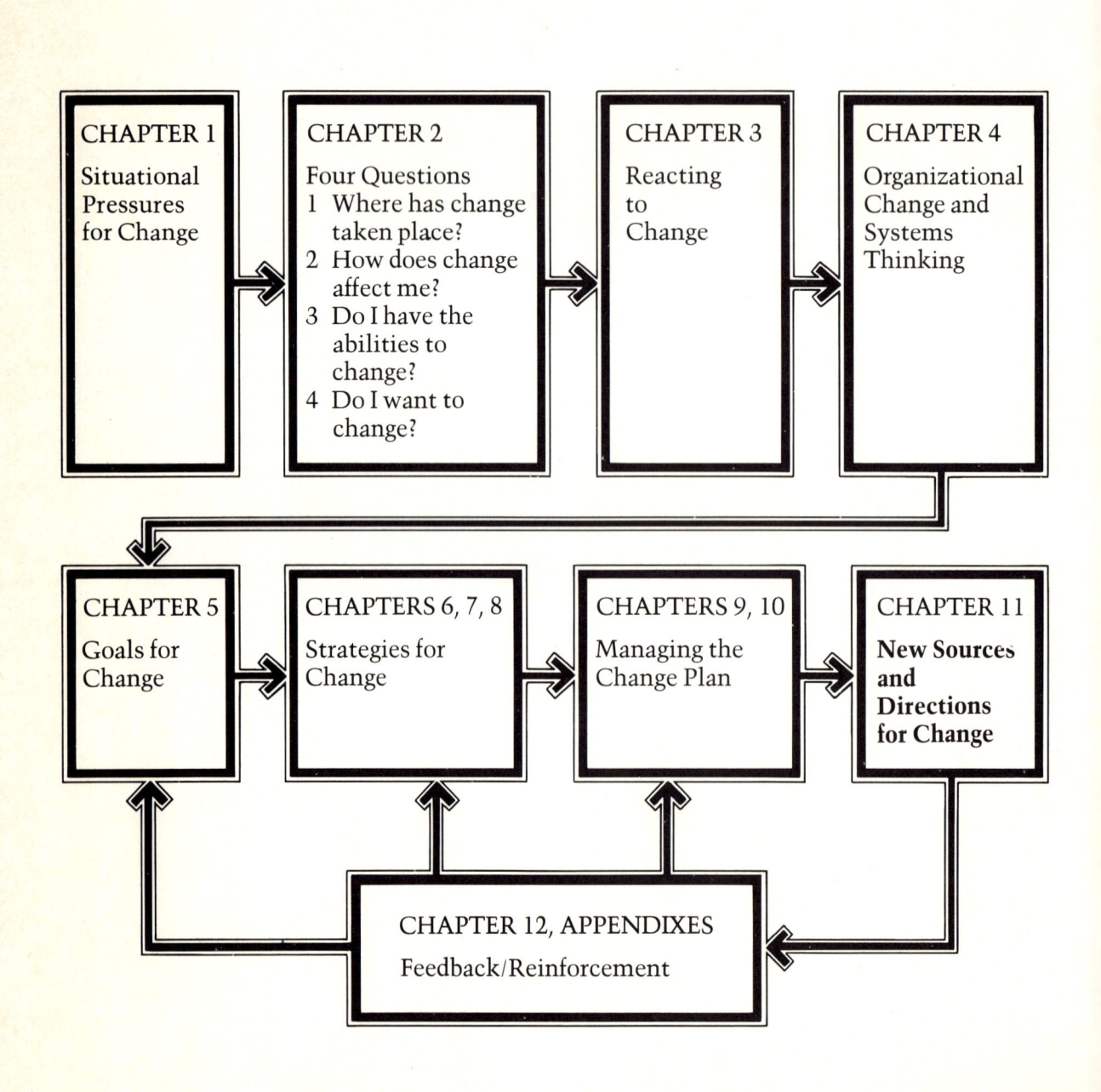

```
┌─────────────┐    ┌──────────────────┐    ┌─────────────┐    ┌─────────────┐
│ CHAPTER 1   │    │ CHAPTER 2        │    │ CHAPTER 3   │    │ CHAPTER 4   │
│             │    │                  │    │             │    │             │
│ Situational │    │ Four Questions   │    │ Reacting    │    │ Organizational│
│ Pressures   │ ⇒  │ 1 Where has change│ ⇒ │ to          │ ⇒  │ Change and  │
│ for Change  │    │   taken place?   │    │ Change      │    │ Systems     │
│             │    │ 2 How does change│    │             │    │ Thinking    │
│             │    │   affect me?     │    │             │    │             │
│             │    │ 3 Do I have the  │    │             │    │             │
│             │    │   abilities to   │    │             │    │             │
│             │    │   change?        │    │             │    │             │
│             │    │ 4 Do I want to   │    │             │    │             │
│             │    │   change?        │    │             │    │             │
└─────────────┘    └──────────────────┘    └─────────────┘    └─────────────┘
```

- **CHAPTER 1** — Situational Pressures for Change
- **CHAPTER 2** — Four Questions
  1. Where has change taken place?
  2. How does change affect me?
  3. Do I have the abilities to change?
  4. Do I want to change?
- **CHAPTER 3** — Reacting to Change
- **CHAPTER 4** — Organizational Change and Systems Thinking
- **CHAPTER 5** — Goals for Change
- **CHAPTERS 6, 7, 8** — Strategies for Change
- **CHAPTERS 9, 10** — Managing the Change Plan
- **CHAPTER 11** — **New Sources and Directions for Change**
- **CHAPTER 12, APPENDIXES** — Feedback/Reinforcement

A new and growing force for change—the credentialing movement—cannot be ignored. It promises to affect the work lives of thousands of managers, specialists, and professionals. This chapter will clarify some of the major issues and developments of the movement through discussion of its scope, background, and effects. Following this, we turn to practical ways you can deal with the personal impact of credentialing, drawing on the material that has been developed in previous chapters.

What Credentialing Means

Credentialing is an awkward term that refers to establishing or certifying an individual's level of competence (knowledge, skills, and experience) against a standardized body of information and accomplishment. The credentialing process is administered by professional societies, government units, and/or organizations formed or designed for these purposes.

Since credentialing is not a remote, future possibility but is a here-and-now fact, an ongoing *change*, it may well constitute a significant area of concern for you. Regardless of your need at this point, it is likely that credentialing will enter your life in some way and will serve as a catalyst for change.

Credentialing Then . . .

Traditionally, public protection, legal considerations, or the furtherance of public interest provided key reasons for the licensing and regulation of various specialty or professional groups. The medical field is illustrative of these developments. High visibility and life and death considerations helped to establish regulation in the health field. Yet even under these compelling circumstances, successful regulation came slowly. Problems encountered involved political jurisdictions, resistance by professionals, public apathy, and a general distrust by many of regulation and the regulatory bodies themselves. Some of the very same factors are associated with current credentialing movements.

... And Now

Some credentialing developments have come about as attempts to regulate the labor supply or establish self-governance. Matters of legal liability also sparked credentialing in various fields. But recent developments in credentialing have occurred for other than health, safety, or legal reasons.

Business, government, and the scientific world have become increasingly complex, calling for levels of occupational specialization or creating wholly new specialties without precedent. For example, technological change has grown almost exponentially. The advent of computerization or automation is only the visual shift reflecting a whole new era of scientific personnel of every description who have created, programmed, or managed these changes. Too, competition in the business world has become more intense and varied, reflecting substitutable products or services, many countries of origin, and organizational forms such as the conglomerate, which span many industries. Thus there has been a need to foster a whole new group of forecasters, planners, analysts, and coordinators. These new professionals have assumed new roles in monitoring the environment for change, forecasting the thrust of change, and helping to introduce change.

In the management of complex organizations or the supervision of human resources, traditional bureaucratic or management principles have given way to new practices and approaches based on the management and behavioral sciences. Similar directions could be described for specific industries, such as insurance and banking, and occupations involving the sale of real estate and manufacturing engineering.

A Personnel Example

A research study on professionalization carried out at Arizona State University in 1975 listed over fifty credentialing groups, many new since 1950, as suggestive of the scope of this movement.

In the case of the personnel field, a vast series of environmental changes resulted in a whole new fabric of legislative regulation, as well as recognition of the need for better planning and management of human resources. Equal Employment Opportunity (EEO), Occupational Safety and Health (OSHA), and Employee Retirement and Insurance (ERISA) considerations represent just a few of the many new legal developments requiring a pronounced change in personnel activities. Accurate and complete knowledge of the new legislation, planning tools, improved techniques for gaining employee motivation and commitment, and new approaches to analysis were among the requirements emerging for personnel specialists.

In connection with all this, various personnel members were assuming heavier and key responsibilities. Personnel managers and specialists were being increasingly called upon to provide counsel and analysis or to make policy recommendations for new lines of human resource actions.

More was being demanded of individuals bearing the personnel title. In addition, new specialties were being created with titles such as manpower forecaster, career planner, organization development manager, and affirmative action officer.

A credentialing program was finally set up in 1975 by the American Society of Personnel Administrators (ASPA). The momentum of its impact on personnel people grew as it was fed by various public relations efforts and ASPA policy pronouncements. As with most other credentialing efforts, accredited individuals eventually became the best proponents and supporters of the program. By 1978, increasing numbers of individuals were experiencing various degrees of awareness, knowledge, or even commitment to the credentialing idea. However, this program, as with many others, encountered critics both within and without. There was an important, positive side to the criticism to the extent that the assumptions, activities, and general program were carefully scrutinized for relevance to the aims of the credentialing movement.

Impact on Those in Personnel

Continuing education and development have become increasing concerns of the personnel manager and specialist. These established change conditions or fostered individual change. First, job responsibilities of individuals require bringing into play an up-to-date and relevant body of skills and information. Second, the various personnel societies and the academic community have introduced a whole new group of continuing development courses offered in many subjects and almost every conceivable length, location, and format. Continuing education units (CEUs) are provided for course completion, and these in turn may be used for company/organization or credentialing purposes. Third, the pace of the credentialing program has grown and the need with it to (a) prepare oneself for testing, or (b) maintain credentials established previously through testing, or "grandfathering." Fourth, the encouragement of various organizational officials has provided additional program reinforcement. In truth, this support is not wholly altruistic; the individual is seen as gaining in stature. But many organizations also regard credentialing as upgrading of their reputation, as viewed by the public they serve.

Generalizing from the Particular

The growth of credentialing in the personnel field fits in with the change model and concepts presented in earlier chapters.

1 WHERE HAS CHANGE TAKEN PLACE? The winds for change in the personnel field were not detected uniformly by members of the field. In spite of legislative, competitive, social, and economic changes, many thought (and some still think!) in terms of business as usual. Thus for some personnel specialists, the indicated environmental changes were seen as isolated but not especially noteworthy events, perhaps acknowledged as a part of "government control" or interpreted as "competition has always been tough."

2 HOW DOES CHANGE AFFECT ME? Studies of large numbers of personnel officials* indicate that even where significant environmental changes were acknowledged, these officials did not see those changes as directly related to their own abilities: "Yes, we've had to change our information records, the kinds of questions we ask of new applicants and the like, but that's about it." Many of the people who had moved into the personnel field came to it from various other areas of the organization including production, marketing, public relations, and even accounting. Thus, it is not surprising that many lacked formal preparation in the field—and didn't even acknowledge the need for special educational preparation for themselves upon entering the field. The present need, as they saw it, was to meet new procedural requirements on behalf of their company and not to retune personal abilities, orientation, or outlooks. The events that brought about individual confrontation with the changes were manifold:

- Public relations programs of the credentialing body.

- Society meetings given over to the subject.

---

* Professor Edwin Miller of the University of Michigan (in conjunction with Elmer H. Burack) *The Credentialing Movement: A Report on Behalf of the ASPA*. (Berea, Ohio: Accreditation Institute, 1978).

- Talks by senior company officials describing the major changes taking place in their business or organization and the impact on the personnel function.

- Articles in professional journals and general business publications describing the changes taking place.

- Direct observation by the individuals involved as change continued to gather force about them.

3 DO I WANT TO CHANGE? The reasons underlying an individual's felt need or desire to change ranged from implied threat to positive reinforcement to realization of benefits to self. In some organizations, senior managers and officials actively encouraged key people in personnel to go through the credentialing process as a step in keeping with the organization's professional character; this was especially true in public accounting firms. Others who were motivated to seek credentialing saw the new guidelines and field tests as a personal challenge and measure of accomplishment. Still others looked upon credentialing as a safety play: "Don't know when I'll need it or even if I'll need it, but if I change jobs or things change around here, it may come in handy." The opportunity for *grandfathering* undoubtedly influenced a number of individuals to apply with the thought of gaining credentials based on experience, past and current job assignments, and education. The fact that *re*credentialing was required after a three-year period (through demonstration of continuing education) was likely, however, to pose a major personal challenge later in time. As a final point here, it is well to note that for people away from the classroom for many years, reentry into these channels of development was frightening. Yet where colleagues or friends were going through the same thing or where small study groups formed for review purposes, anxious individuals received much support and encouragement.

4 DO I HAVE THE ABILITIES TO CHANGE? As just mentioned, not having been in the classroom for some time posed problems for many. Part of the difficulty was the *uncertainty* of what knowledge or skills would have to be mastered. The provision of study guides and reference tests by the credentialing group helped to meet these questions and in turn to provide some reassurance. It was discovered first of all that the required learning was not insurmountable. Particular bodies of information or skills had to be demonstrated, but these were specific and capable of accomplishment through personal effort. Gaining the new knowledge was thus as much a psychological as a mechanical matter. The *motivation* to change provided the impetus to question *ability* to change. And realization that ability was adequate to the task increased motivation.

Change at Two Levels

Experiences connected with the personnel credentialing program are typical of many other efforts. Change takes place at two distinctly different levels. At one level, the sponsoring organizations are involved and the orientation and direction of their efforts are the change issues. The second level involves individual change—the challenges faced by specialists, managers, and professionals when they are eventually confronted with the need for change as presented to them by a credentialing program.

Rewards Beyond the Pressure

It's easy enough to pay lip service to the reality and impact of the credentialing movement. But change at the personal level—starting down the path to meet credentialing standards—may be less than enthusiastic. This is most likely when motivation rests on outside pressure. But even those who are personally sold on the wisdom of credentialing may be unable to generate very positive reasons beyond the "union card" type of argument.

It would be a mistake, however, to define credentialing in such static terms. The satisfaction that goes along with successfully meeting new situations can provide a tremendous sense of accomplishment. For many this is reward enough. But it doesn't stop there. Better feelings about yourself are a stimulus for further personal change.

The financial side of credentialing can hardly be ignored either. Obviously, there may be immediate gains. In addition, obtaining credentials may of itself constitute a demonstration of individual ability and thus be viewed favorably by others in assessing a person's potential. Improved skills and performance resulting from credentialing efforts may also position an individual for heavier future responsibilities and compensation.

Organizational Gains

From the standpoint of an organization, credentialing activities of professional societies are one of the important means for helping to assure superior performance by organization members. Although there is no guarantee that organizations that choose to support credentialing efforts will benefit, the odds are high that such participation will increase profits.

Credentialing and Your Organization

Are any credentialing activities being considered or taking place under sponsorship of your professional association or group? (WHERE HAS CHANGE OCCURRED?)

_____

_____

If so, how does this activity relate to you? (HOW DOES CHANGE AFFECT ME?) If not, how *might* credentialing affect you and your organization in the future?

_____

_____

continued

Credentialing and Your Organization (continued)

If credentialing is relevant to your position in the sense of personal certification, are you ready to take the necessary steps? (DO I WANT TO CHANGE?) What are these steps?

_____
_____
_____

Do you feel equipped to do so? (DO I HAVE THE ABILITIES TO CHANGE?) List any considerations you may have. _____

_____
_____

If the credentialing movement still seems remote to you or your organization, do the reasons revolve about time lag, organizational resistance, lack of organizational need, or other factors? Elaborate on your impressions.

Credentialing as it affects own organization
_____
_____
_____
_____
_____
_____

Strengthening Professionalism

Keep in mind that the very concept of professionalism is still relatively new as applied to occupations beyond those traditionally defined as professions. An organization committed to increasing its ranks of certified individuals must make its members aware of credentialing needs and programs and demonstrate the *value of change* in this direction. The gathering and distribution of pertinent information is one concrete way to achieve these objectives. Motivation to obtain certification (as well as motivation for continuing identification with a professional body) is also strengthened by a more subtle aspect of the work climate: visible and active participation of key individuals in their respective professional bodies.

Extending Professionalism in Your Organization

The following questions summarize some key factors conducive to extending professionalism in your organization.

1 Does information exist as to the professional affiliations of organization members? Yes ____ No ____

2 Do some organization members carry out roles wholly or partially identified with professional fields, yet maintain no affiliation themselves? Yes ____ No ____

3 Do officials, managers, and professionals themselves identify with various professional societies and/or fields? Yes ____ No ____

4 Have organization members developed collegial ties based on areas of technical or administrative competency? Yes ____ No ____

5 Do you and others in the organization have some idea of the professionally related reading, education, and other development activities of relevant organization members? Yes ____ No ____

6 Do bases exist to determine the accessibility of organization members to needed sources of knowledge and skill development? Yes ____ No ____

In Brief

The credentialing movement is a current force for change. Unlike more traditional certification practices, the present movement affects *large* numbers of members in *all types* of organizations. It may be understood as a response to ever-increasing knowledge, specialization, and organizational complexity, and corresponding needs to upgrade competency of organization members; to regulate and protect organizational and professional interests; and to facilitate compliance with government legislation related to the public interest.

Some issues at the organizational and personal levels are common to credentialing efforts in all occupational fields. These concern the change orientation of professional societies and the uncertainties and fears faced by individuals under pressure to achieve certification.

Individual readiness to meet credentialing needs may be analyzed in relationship to the four question change model. Although credentialing motivation is often focused on immediate gains, future profits to both individuals and organizations may be substantial.

In the concluding chapter we will touch again on what we think it is most important to know about change.

Action Checklist

1   Can you identify present organization members who have been or are likely to be affected by credentialing activities? Yes ____ No ____

2   Does management perceive how growing professionalism relates to the needs of the organization? Yes ____ No ____

3   Do specific means exist to monitor and analyze the impact for organization members as fields of knowledge change? Yes ____ No ____

4   Is there general acknowledgement of the organization's responsibility in support of individual relevance, managerial or professional titles notwithstanding? Yes ____ No ____

5   Are individuals acknowledging their personal responsibility for updating and maintaining knowledge and skill relevance? Yes ____ No ____

6   Does the organization draw on the credentialing movement or knowledge of growing professionalism as a strategy for encouraging individual change? Yes ____ No ____

Summing Up— and Looking Ahead 12

Permanence may be only a fiction.

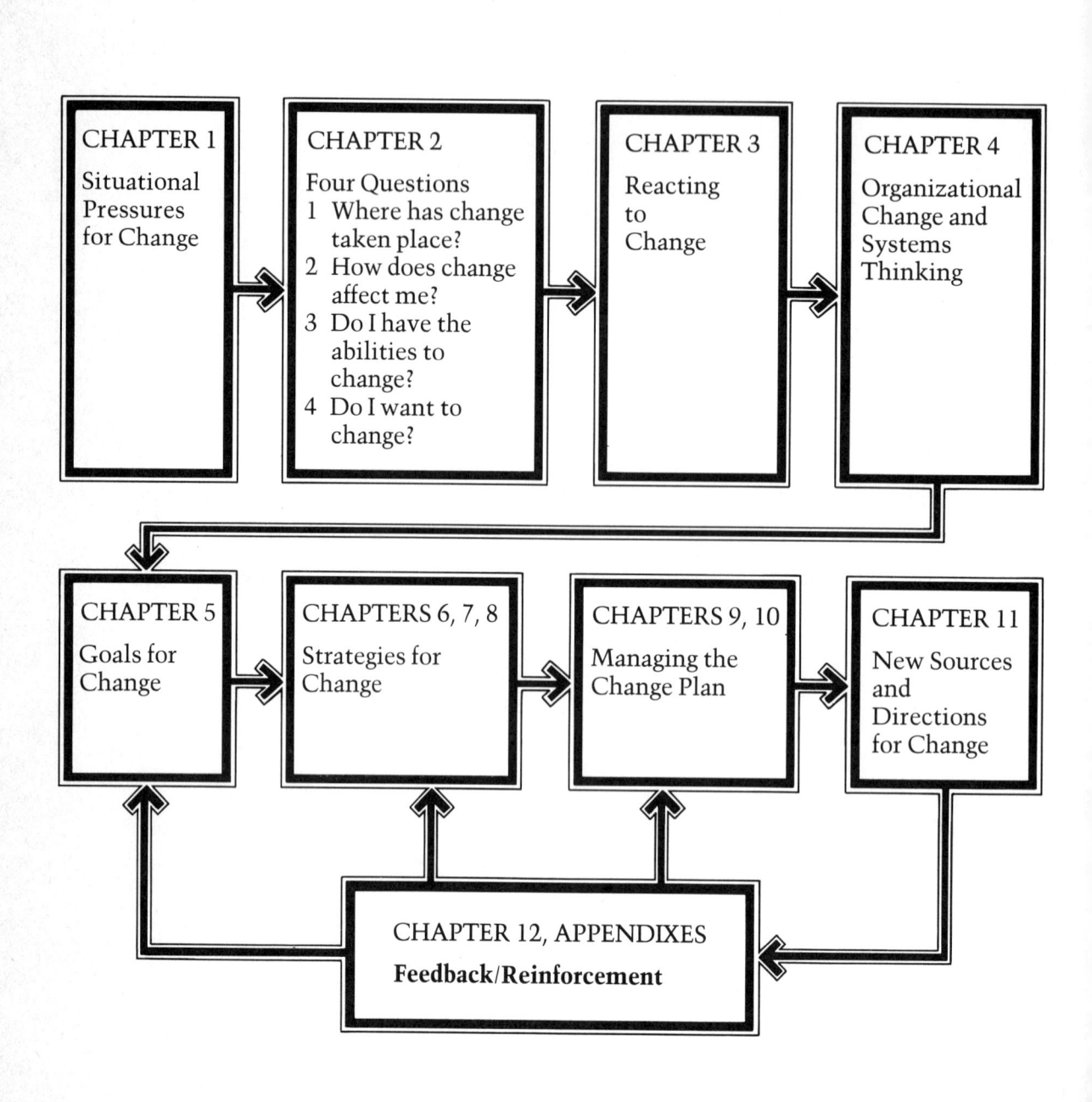

CHAPTER 1	CHAPTER 2	CHAPTER 3	CHAPTER 4
Situational Pressures for Change	Four Questions 1 Where has change taken place? 2 How does change affect me? 3 Do I have the abilities to change? 4 Do I want to change?	Reacting to Change	Organizational Change and Systems Thinking

CHAPTER 5	CHAPTERS 6, 7, 8	CHAPTERS 9, 10	CHAPTER 11
Goals for Change	Strategies for Change	Managing the Change Plan	New Sources and Directions for Change

CHAPTER 12, APPENDIXES
Feedback/Reinforcement

Change. We hope that the word strikes you differently by now—that it calls forth new definitions and interpretations, and more confident attitudes toward what you can do to help yourself and others accept, create, or even reject change for positive reasons.

Change may be deeply troubling, and we have not tried to explain it away through the argument that nothing in nature remains fixed. Permanence may be only a fiction, yet acceptance of this doesn't necessarily make change easier.

Nor have we taken the position that change is best understood as dramatic or disturbing discontinuity between today and yesterday or today and the future. Unquestionably some change is of that order. But people are too inclined to perceive change as "happening overnight," when in truth it is more gradual. Instead, our approach has been to avoid definitions of what is "real" change, where change starts and stops, or the kinds of change that make an important difference. We believe that dependence on other peoples' definitions is part of the problem in dealing with change.

Change is most productively conceived as what you perceive it to be. Because the world is changing all along, change can therefore begin anywhere you please. A traumatic change is often due simply to the failure to spot its antecedents. This process of selection is not, however, just the pure exercise of unlimited choice. You may paint your own picture of change, but the results (your choices) will reflect the materials and techniques available and known to you, as well as your conceptions of what a picture should include. Denial of certain knowledge or experience—when it is difficult to reconcile with what you believe or desire—may also influence this process.

We have made a case for developing the personal resources that determine the manner in which you live with or take hold of ongoing change. All change issues can be seen as arising in an organizational setting (in some network of patterned activities and responsibilities), but our focus has been on the *individual's* capacity to handle change in ways conducive to personal satisfaction and achievement. This includes managerial obligations to plan for and bring about change in others.

Whether, What, and How to Change

Adequacy related to change includes resources for both diagnosis (how to think about the issue) and action (how to change in some way oneself, other individuals, or groups). The table on p. 199 lists topics previously discussed and illustrates how they contribute to these resources. Various points are amplified in the discussion below.

Four Basic Questions

Our change model, consisting of four basic questions, points to areas where trouble about change originates, or insight may be gained:

WHERE HAS CHANGE TAKEN PLACE?

This question directs your attention to a broader range of events than those customarily observed. By taking a more comprehensive view of personal, organizational, community, and worldwide matters you are not so apt to experience change as a series of unrelated and abrupt surprises; you are also more likely to perceive or anticipate connections between the changes in various spheres of activity.

HOW DOES CHANGE AFFECT ME?

With fuller awareness of general change, you can then consider how it may eventually affect your own circumstances. You can weigh options and develop strategies to accommodate changes imposed (defined) by others. You are less likely to respond with feelings of helplessness and frustration. Creative leadership is dependent on the ability to grasp future connections among seemingly unrelated events and to act on this awareness in charting organizational change.

Developing Resources for Dealing with Change

TOPIC

Diagnosis ←	How contributes to	→ Action
Where does change present problems?	**Four Question Change Model**	Best points of intervention
Understanding resistance and acceptance of change as it intersects all areas of life	**General Knowledge of Change Dynamics**	Choosing change strategies (changing circumstances; changing people)
Fuller knowledge leading to more objective conclusions	**Systems Thinking**	Choosing among options related to change; setting priorities; long-range planning
Questioning of goals reveals contradictions, discrepancies, and so forth	**Goal Clarification**	Rejection, confirmation, modification, or development of new goals; goal structuring to facilitate achievement
Sensitivity to total organization performance, systems effects, uneven time requirements for change	**Organization Development**	Development of comprehensive framework for change programs; effective collaboration with outside consultants
Questioning of personal beliefs; analyzing organization policies in terms of underlying biases	**Organization Policies**	Change-conscious inputs to policy formulation and correction

continued

Developing Resources for Dealing with Change (continued)

TOPIC

Diagnosis ←	How contributes to	→ Action
Assessment of whether new areas of expertise bear on organizational change and if members have such knowledge and related credentials	← **Credentialing** →	Selection of appropriate measures for promoting and supporting efforts to increase professionalism

DO I HAVE THE ABILITIES TO CHANGE?

Effective response to change may be impeded by lack of abilities or *fear* that you cannot learn what is required. Clarification of these problems through concrete information and well-planned skill development both reduces resistance to change and paves the way for further self-development.

DO I WANT TO CHANGE?

Motivation and ability are related aspects of readiness to change. Strong motivation may be the impetus for developing new skills, and a sense of personal adequacy may enhance motivation for change. This important connection between motivation and ability is, of course, only one facet of motivation.

Applying the Questions

The four basic questions in our change model help to locate where individuals, subunits, or entire organizations have special difficulties with respect to change and whether such difficulties are even perceived as bearing on their problems. You may be unaware, for example, that lack of curiosity about innovation within your own organization hinders your chances for a position elsewhere. Or your organization may not recognize how little it is tuned in to community affairs, which are nevertheless affecting your organization's local market. Analysis along each of these four dimensions of change goes beyond diagnosis to suggest appropriate points of intervention.

Systems Thinking

Systems thinking is a tool for confronting change-related issues or problems, especially where managerial responsibilities are concerned. Systems thinking allows for testing and extending your own view of a situation in order to develop effective strategies for action.

Briefly, systems thinking is a way of looking at the change problem or need, its origins, scope, and effects throughout the organization both from your own point of view and the point of view of others. This approach corrects for personal error in defining and evaluating a situation. It expands awareness of the system (organization) both as a whole and as a set of mutually dependent internal relationships.

Systems thinking dispels the myth of "final" or "objective" knowledge. It makes clear that circumstances outside the system create ever new goal dilemmas; that each subunit must deal with different aspects of these overall goals; and that each level of responsibility creates different pressures. Moreover, systems thinking recognizes that there is variation in human reactions. Change cannot be successfully planned or implemented without taking into consideration various perspectives and needs internal to the system and recognizing that the system itself must remain responsive to change in the larger society.

Both the four question change model and systems thinking are most useful as ways of checking yourself and tracking events. As habits of mind, they reveal both problem areas and opportunities related to change and the direction for action.

Rethinking Goals

Systems thinking is especially likely to bring goals under sharper scrutiny. The goals may be questioned in terms of their validity for the organization as a whole and in terms of what they represent to various segments of an organization. Once clarified, goals may be reformulated to make change in their direction both feasible and desirable.

Sensitivity to Motivational Factors   Preparing yourself or others for change is easier with an understanding of the many and sometimes far from obvious circumstances that condition motivation. Resistance to a given change is often due to considerations that have nothing to do with the change itself. When resistance relates directly to a change, it is well to remember that the reasons may be rational and sensible. Resistance is not in itself wrong. In addition, it is helpful to recognize that attitudes toward change are frequently mixed, rather than purely positive or negative. This means that positive elements, if appealed to, may serve as a natural ally in promoting change.

Ways to Promote Change   By concentrating on the manager's needs to carry through or plan for organizational change, we made a distinction between creating *circumstances* conducive to change in others and attempts to influence *basic attitudes* of others. The strategies we discussed within each framework bring to attention significant forces in the service of change. Because many of these are not ordinarily examined in connection with change, this therefore permits thinking about change in new ways.

Taking Action

It should be clear by now that there is no single formula for guiding change. Armed with increased insight and tools, you must still juggle a great many facts of organizational life in devising a workable set of strategies. Naturally there is wide variation in the nature and magnitude of the change task. But each manager must also deal with the constraints connected with a particular organization, a particular set of roles and responsibilities, and finally the personal traits of a particular group of people!

Although you must find your own way to cope with the unique circumstances you face, the path will be easier once you review those circumstances. For example, the size of your organization is probably the most conspicuous characteristic. But other qualities are equally important to think about as they relate to options for promoting change. Is the organization fairly stable or is it rapidly changing? What is its history (and success) in regard to undertaking change? Do technical constraints limit innovation? Does the organization tend to take a supportive, neutral, or antagonistic position toward the proposals of managerial personnel? What are its traditional patterns of procedure, its characteristic ways of doing things?

Next, consider roles and responsibilities. How many administrative levels are associated with the change task? What are the levels at which responsibility is assumed for people and for resources? An extremely important question concerns the relationship between official roles and unofficial power—who has the "real" power? In planning for change at any level, it is unrealistic to ignore the politics of the situation.

Finally, examine personal traits. Is there skilled leadership? What is the *style* of formal leadership? What other qualities of individual personality bear on the change task? What is the state of health of key people? Do they have a history of successful change? Is age relevant?

The answers to these questions may seem to complicate matters, but they *also* suggest ways to proceed.

Scaling Up Designing change programs has much in common at different levels of accountability. Effectiveness in any situation requires a well informed diagnosis of needs and selection of suitable means for achieving goals. The management of large-scale change necessarily involves greater coordination and a more extensive information base, but all principles and approaches that have been discussed are consistent with more ambitious requirements.

Contributing to Organizational Policy Those who help make the rules may unknowingly work against strengthening an organization's capacity for change. Since personal philosophies find their way into the setting of organizational policy, it is important to question their relevance to change.

How do assumptions about human nature, the meaning of work, and what is "good" for an organization translate into regulations and procedures governing recruitment and selection of employees, content and scope of training sponsored by the organization, degree of participation in decision-making, planning as a routine or sporadic activity, and even policy that supports or denies the very need for change? Do these practices in turn square with longer-range goals for organizational development? As with individuals, organizations stand to profit from discovering, questioning, and rethinking the hidden premises on which their policies are based.

The Credentialing Movement

Social and technological change increasingly call for new forms of expertise in organizational administration. Computer automation, the "new work ethic," and women in management are but a few instances of the major changes taking place. This leads to various paths of specialization and poses organizational questions related to standardization of job requirements and provisions for necessary training. In a growing number of fields, professional organizations are assuming the responsibilities for developing and sponsoring certification programs. Even those individuals who have so far been relatively sheltered from organizational change cannot afford to ignore this current and extremely significant movement. The credentialing movement means that managers can expect to experience both new pressures and new opportunities for change. These may revolve about determining what areas of specialization are relevant to organizational needs and then taking steps leading to certification. Preparation for this type of change must be concerned with motivation and reassurance, as well as with practical arrangements for appropriate training.

Changed Conceptions of Change

The ability to perceive change in less explosive increments and in more far-reaching terms, provides greater control over events. But keep in mind that not everyone will view change this way. As a manager you should be alert to the host of reasons for resistance to change. Such knowledge leads to better planning for implementing change and pays off in terms of goodwill and increased cooperation.

You should further be able to relate change to all manner of often mundane activities, that is, the effect of day-to-day events on yourself and others. This reveals what "works" to modify behavior. Various types of influence, sometimes subtle, sometimes not, continually set the stage for change. The deliberate promotion of change requires awareness of the role and modes of influence and judicious application. These means for encouraging change are neutral—influence may be turned to all sorts of purposes—but you should now also be in a better position to question any goals in terms of whose and what interests they serve. What kind of change do they stand for?

Change is not automatic progress, and we have not advocated change for the sake of change. Up-to-dateness is not the issue. Progress, however, does imply development, or *constructive change*. What we have been concerned with is defusing the concept of change and spelling out its ramifications in order to help you further your own ideas of progress.

Count on Waves and Ripples

In *judging* your progress, along whatever lines the situation calls for, don't lose sight of—and if need be, comfort yourself with—a final truth: Once set in motion, change in and of itself will continue to have ongoing consequences. Some of these will be delayed, remote, and perhaps even indeterminate. The practical import of all this is for you to take the longer and wider view of change, as we have urged all along.

Appendix I: Ideas and Guidelines from the Change Literature

Research in the change management process is by no means comprehensive. Nevertheless, enough has been published to be of significant use to management practitioners. This annotated bibliography contains a representative cross section of literature that can be useful in particular situations calling for individual or organizational change.

In the table on p. 208, the selected readings are organized around the four questions that have served in this book to highlight major considerations bearing on change. The numbered entries correspond to the publication summaries in this appendix.

Four-Question Change Model Applied to Relevant Change Literature

WHERE HAS CHANGE TAKEN PLACE?	HOW DOES CHANGE AFFECT ME/US?
Individual Level	
1 Pearse & Pelzer	1 Pearse & Pelzer
2 Hall	2 Hall
3 Burack & Smith	3 Burack & Smith
12 Humble	8 Cetron
	10 Luft
	11 Golembiewski & Blumberg
	12 Humble
	22 Lippitt
Organizational Level	
3 Burack & Smith	3 Burack & Smith
4 French & Bell	4 French & Bell
5 Dyer	5 Dyer
6 Nadler	6 Nadler
7 Burack & Mathys	7 Burack & Mathys
8 Cetron	8 Cetron
9 Beckhard & Harris	9 Beckhard & Harris
21 Davis & Lawrence	13 Rogers & Rogers
	21 Davis & Lawrence
	22 Lippitt

continued

Ideas and Guidelines from the Change Literature

DO I/WE WANT TO CHANGE?	**DO I/WE HAVE THE ABILITIES TO CHANGE?**
Individual Level	
12 Humble	10 Luft
14 Steers & Porter	11 Golembiewski & Blumberg
15 The Conference Board	17 Mager & Pipe
16 Herzberg	18 Rockey
22 Lippitt	19 Saint
Organizational Level	
4 French & Bell	4 French & Bell
5 Dyer	5 Dyer
6 Nadler	6 Nadler
14 Steers & Porter	13 Rogers & Rogers
15 The Conference Board	17 Mager & Pipe
16 Herzberg	19 Saint
22 Lippitt	20 Stockhard
	21 Davis & Lawrence

1 *Self-Directed Change for the Mid Career Manager* by Robert F. Pearse and B. Purdy Pelzer. New York: Amacom, A Division of the American Management Associations, 1975.

Mid-career should be a time of new challenge and personal growth. Your personal growth can be considerably enhanced by intensive self-examination of the events and forces that have shaped your life to date. Recognizing that the hardest part of this analysis may be getting started, Pearse and Pelzer provide in this book practical tools for personal growth through self-analysis and self-directed change.

Guidelines for change are presented in the following areas: (1) the manager's current position, organizational dynamics, interpersonal relations, and career effects; (2) the manager's off-the-job world: family, friends, and community; (3) a social history summary of what has happened in the lifetimes of managers currently in mid-career; (4) a Managerial Mid-Career Balance Sheet and an Action Plan for self-directed change.

Also included are twenty-five brief case histories of managers at mid-career to enable you to evaluate your past career and to plan the most likely, beneficial future moves.

2 *Careers in Organizations* by Douglas T. Hall. Santa Monica, Calif.: Goodyear Publishing Co., 1976.

A "career" may be understood as the individually perceived sequence of attitudes and behaviors associated with work-related experiences and activities over the span of a person's life. Hall deals with some of the most significant questions attaching to the career concept: How do people choose their careers? What factors make for career success or failure? And how can organizations help individuals in developing their careers more successfully?

The author reports on devices for career self-improvement. One example is the Self-Directed Search, a

Ideas and Guidelines from the Change Literature

psychological instrument for producing a profile of vocational preference and career orientation. Another example is a process offered by Educational Testing Service for self-diagnosis of career-related values with the aid of an on-line interactive computer, which directs the individual to information on a wide variety of occupations.

The author believes it is crucial that the organization not thrust the burden of career success entirely on the individual. He offers a number of basic suggestions for organizational supportive action including better employee-position matchups during initial hiring, monitoring performance progress more imaginatively, and reshaping the employer's role to that of a career developer.

3 "Personnel Management Information Systems," Chapter 15 in *Personnel Management* by Elmer H. Burack and Robert D. Smith. St. Paul, Minn.: West Publishing Company, 1977.

Advancing computer technology and the availability of more sophisticated tools of analysis have made many traditional approaches to personnel management outdated. The authors provide materials to develop an appreciation of the wide gaps that exist among existing personnel methods, human needs in organizations, and available computer technology. Also examined are the design and evaluation components of personnel management information systems (PMIS) as these apply to decision-making and reporting requirements. Contemporary uses of the PMIS concept are included, as are the implications of information systems for future developments in the personnel field.

The PMIS concept and managing change are strongly interrelated. Through use of such a system, the effect of environmental trends on human resources may be monitored. Simultaneously, changes in the internal composition of an organization's work force may be tracked, both on an individual basis and by employment classifications. The authors include a number of case examples to illustrate the potentials and the pitfalls of PMIS implementation.

4 *Organization Development* by Wendell French and Cecil H. Bell, Jr. Englewood Cliffs, N.J.: Prentice-Hall, 1973 (paperback).

Through an economic writing style and judicious use of figures, tables, and exhibits, French and Bell provide comprehensive coverage of OD as a change strategy. Proceeding from a definition of Organization Development and a sketch of its historical antecedents, the authors identify the key process elements of OD as well as the assumptions and value judgments of its advocates and practitioners.

The focus of the book, however, is on alternative applications of OD methods, or to use the authors' language, the various OD "interventions" into ongoing activities of an organization. Interventions can take place on three levels: individual, group, and total organization. Individuals can be affected, for example, through sensitivity training or career counseling. The behavior and activities of groups can be affected by team building, diagnostic meetings, and/or role analysis techniques. At the total organization level, "confrontation" meetings, attitude survey feedback, and "managerial grid" programs can all be used to bring about change.

French and Bell also itemize the conditions needed for optimal success with OD processes, the issues and problems typically encountered, and conclude by addressing the question of whether OD will be a passing fad.

5 *Team Building: Issues and Alternatives* by William G. Dyer. Reading, Mass.: Addison-Wesley Publishing Co., 1977 (paperback).

"Team building" as a way of implementing Organization Development is grounded on the observation that more and more managers are working collectively and collaboratively in the handling of organizational problems. This trend places a premium on interpersonal and collaborative skills, in which many managers are deficient.

Dyer writes for the practicing manager who is interested in how to design and conduct a program of team development. He warns that team development is not a panacea for organizational problems but rather a long-range effort to unite people in the improvement of organizational functioning.

Major topics include: methods of team development; team development as a change strategy; team development as a data-gathering, diagnostic, and action-planning process; the team building cycle; and roles played in the team development process. Attention is also paid to such special problems as interteam conflict, and conflict between "the boss" and the rest of the team. Illustrative case studies are placed effectively throughout the book.

6 *Feedback and Organization Development: Using Data-Based Methods* by David A. Nadler. Reading, Mass.: Addison-Wesley Publishing Co., 1977 (paperback).

Nadler concentrates on the vital roles played by data and communication in the initiation, management, and stabilization of the change process. He deals with a wide range of questions and issues concerning the various methods for gathering data, organizing and learning from it, as well as alternative modes of feedback to organization members.

After presenting a model of data collection and feedback, the author discusses how information changes behavior, then goes on to detailed coverage of data collection and analysis techniques: interviews, questionnaires, observations, and secondary data, with summaries of their advantages and limitations. Nadler also provides an excellent section on the design and conduct of the feedback process, including alternative methods that can be drawn upon. He concludes with a discussion of likely new directions for future, data-based OD interventions.

7 *Human Resource Planning: Staffing Vol. I, Career Management Vol. II.* by Elmer H. Burack and Nicholas Mathys. Lake Forest, Ill.: Brace-Park Press, 1980.

The authors develop a framework for understanding the effective use of human resources in organizations. They also provide a practical apparatus for the analysis and resolution of specific human resource problems at the operating level. To these ends Burack and Mathys first present the arguments in favor of human resource programming as a deliberate organizational policy, then proceed to specify the planning, auditing, forecasting, and programming components of an overall human resource model.

Particular attention is paid to computer-based methods. System boundaries are also discussed, as are procedures for matching organizational manpower needs with labor market information.

The authors make frequent use of case studies from their own research to aid the reader in moving from planning and programming concepts to their specific applications.

8 *Technological Forecasting* by Marvin J. Cetron. New York: Gordon and Breach, Science Publishers, 1971.

Any type of forecasting is usually regarded as a complex undertaking, fraught with risk and best left to experts. Marvin Cetron sets out to improve on this situation by promoting the use of a logical system that, when applied to technology data, can result in credible and explicit predictions concerning specific technological developments. He draws heavily upon his experiences with the U.S. Department of Defense, where he feels the most progress has been made in the forecasting field.

Major topics include: the purposes of technological forecasts; the structure and content of forecasts; alternative methods of deriving forecasts (e.g., by the extrapolation of past trends); research-and-development forecasting; measuring technological change; choosing methods for forecasting technological change; and putting forecasts to work by the allocation of organizational resources.

The author also provides a survey of quantitative methods relevant to the whole discussion of forecasting, as well as numerous helpful exhibits, flowcharts, and graphs.

9 *Organizational Transitions: Managing Complex Change* by Richard Beckhard and Reuben T. Harris. Reading, Mass.: Addison-Wesley Publishing Co., 1977 (paperback).

Beckhard and Harris address, as a primary audience, managers significantly involved with managing the design and planning the future of their organizations. They base their views on experiences as management consultants and academic researchers.

The authors first describe the thought processes needed to define an organization's current state, identifying sources of needed change and specifying the desired future state after changes have been accomplished. The next stage requires management of the *transition* between the present and the future. Questions dealt with include: Where in the organization should change begin? What intervention method should be used? What management mechanisms may aid the transition process?

Guidelines are provided for formulating a "process plan" (a timetable of events during the change period) and for developing a "commitment plan" (a series of steps to secure the support of those people essential to the success of the change). In the latter portion of the book, the authors turn to the evaluation of change success, describing the development of an evaluation plan and its application through a case study.

10 *Of Human Interaction* by Joseph Luft. Palo Alto, Calif.: National Press Books, 1969 (paperback).

Growth and development in individual self-awareness is the basic theme Luft pursues. Material is organized around a concept known as the "Johari Window," which divides psychological reality into four major areas: the "open area" of which both the individual and others are aware; the "blind area" of which others are aware but the individual is not; the "hidden area," which the individual conceals from others; and the "unknown area," which is not in the conscious awareness of either the individual or of others.

Through interpersonal action and with the opportunity to draw upon a skilled resource person, the individual can grow psychologically through enlargement of the "open area." This means individuals are expected to let others know them in greater depth, to communicate honestly, and to aid others in expanding their "open areas."

The author examines the "games" people play during group interaction and how these may be understood. In a final section, he applies individual growth and group processes to the development of enhanced leadership capabilities and behavior.

11 *Sensitivity Training and the Laboratory Approach*, 2d ed., edited by Robert T. Golembiewski and Arthur Blumberg. Itasca, Ill.: F. E. Peacock, Publishers, 1973 (paperback).

This volume is organized around four major emphases: (1) a basic learning strategy known as "sensitivity training" or the "laboratory approach," (2) various learning vehicles, such as the "T-group," (3) concepts that relate group processes to individual learning outcomes; and (4) ways in which the laboratory approach can be applied at the plant, in the office, within a hospital, or wherever.

The reader new to these areas as well as the advanced student will find much of value regarding what actually happens during T-group experiences, the various roles people play and the implications of these roles for self-learning and growth, where T-group dynamics can be considered for use, and the current status of sensitivity and laboratory approaches.

12 *Management by Objectives in Action* by John W. Humble. New York: McGraw-Hill Book Co., 1970.

This book is intended to help anyone who is planning to introduce management by objectives (MBO) into an organization. The author's description of both the benefits and difficulties will be helpful to anyone as yet uncommitted to MBO. His presentation is well balanced between case studies of accomplishments and controversial viewpoints and unresolved problems.

The material is organized around a series of questions, which include: What is MBO? Does it work in practice? What specific benefits and difficulties have various organizations experienced with MBO? How are the objectives set? How are managers trained in MBO implementation? How can progress with MBO be measured?

Illustrations of MBO in such areas as marketing and research and development are given. Relationships are also identified between MBO and such organization activities as the setting of business objectives and management manpower planning.

13 *Communication in Organizations* by Everett M. Rogers and Rekha Agarwala-Rogers. New York: The Free Press, 1976 (paperback).

The authors believe that communication is the most vital ingredient in organizational functioning. Without communication, they feel, there would be no organization. In pursuit of these convictions, they have attempted in this book to achieve a concise synthesis of the best available communication research. By so doing, they have advanced the field of organizational communication, providing it with much needed clarity and cohesion.

The book investigates the interconnections between organizational structure and communication, between communication and the quality of organizational climate, and between communication, innovation, and organizational change. Furthermore, concepts and procedures are introduced for the conduct of communication network analyses, for understanding and charting the communication dynamics of working groups, and for the tracking of "grapevines." Extensive use is made of case studies.

14 *Motivation and Work Behavior* by Richard M. Steers and Lyman W. Porter. New York: McGraw-Hill Book Co., 1975.

Steers and Porter accomplish three significant goals: (1) overviews of the most consequential theories of motivation, as these apply to work situations; (2) broad-scale coverage of central, contemporary issues regarding work motivation; and (3) an evaluative summary of what is known about work motivation.

Practicing managers will find the long section devoted to work motivation issues especially valuable. Included are such matters as the relationships between employee morale and productivity; the building of employee loyalty; achieving change acceptance by work groups; the supervisor as a motivator; analyses of leadership goals and means of achieving these; job design, redesign, and employee performance; results-oriented performance evaluations; and money as a motivator. The final chapter contains excellent guidelines for managers to use in managing of motivational processes.

15 *Appraising Managerial Performance.* New York: The Conference Board, 1977 (paperback).

This is a research report based upon questionnaire responses from 293 United States corporations. It provides an excellent overview of current management performance appraisals. Included are the objectives of various appraisal systems, the content of appraisals, description of the selection and training of appraisers, as well as evaluation of the effectiveness of performance appraisals in general.

Thirty-two exhibits of actual appraisal forms plus accompanying commentaries provide specific guidelines for use by other organizations. While the focus is upon the manager's performance, application to other categories of employees can also be made. All the tools for the start-up of an appraisal system are presented here in very understandable terms.

16 *The Managerial Choice* by Frederick Herzberg. Homewood, Ill.: Dow Jones-Irwin, 1976.

This is the author's fourth book on man and his work. In the preceding three, the emphasis was on research findings and theory. This time the focus is on practical applications.

Herzberg believes that jobs and work systems should be designed so as to provide employees with intrinsic challenges. After laying a groundwork he calls "the proper management of employee motivation," he turns to a detailed presentation of his views on "job enrichment." Included are several case histories illustrating job enrichment in diverse settings and research evidence to the effect that job enrichment pays off. The case histories are sufficiently explicit to enable interested managers to export the methodology to new situations. The author rounds out the book with a treatment of the connection between employee job motivation and mental health.

17 *Analyzing Performance Problems* by Robert F. Mager and Peter Pipe. Belmont, Calif.: Fearon-Pitman, Publishers, 1970 (paperback).

In this small book, Mager and Pipe proceed step by step in the analysis of employee performance deficiencies, as seen from the management standpoint. Their interest is, basically, to learn *why* there is a deficiency, *what sort* of deficiency it is, and then what might be done to remedy it.

The authors provide a useful flowchart of thought processes and relevant questions as these apply to performance analyses and consequent action. The chart is particularly helpful in distinguishing performance failures due to inadequate or obsolete training from failures due to other factors, such as faulty motivation. Once the nature of performance failures is understood, Mager and Pipe offer helpful hints for the programming of corrective action.

18 *Communicating in Organizations* by Edward H. Rockey. Cambridge, Mass.: Winthrop Publishers, 1977 (paperback).

Managers spend virtually their entire time at work communicating. To the extent that a manager communicates with consistent effectiveness, his or her career is enhanced. To the extent the reverse is true, his or her career is damaged. The author focuses on various communication improvement goals, such as choosing appropriate message media, organizing messages meaningfully, becoming a better listener, encouraging and making use of feedback, and participating effectively in meetings.

He makes skillful use of developmental exercises to motivate the reader to improve his or her own communication capabilities. Included are exercises aimed at becoming a more effective committee member, a more informative and convincing report writer, and a more efficient user of resource materials. Overall, the author provides a handy workbook for individual improvement of communications skills.

19 *Learning at Work* by Avice Saint. Chicago: Nelson-Hall Co., 1974.

The objective of this book is to describe what must happen in an organization if the organization and its employees are to learn and to carry out their work roles effectively. The author relies primarily upon her research in four private corporations and two federal agencies to build a framework for the development of employee training systems, and to detail the interconnections between these systems and the mainsprings of organizational activities.

The key research finding is that the most productive results occur when training is made part of action needed to solve real organizational problems and accomplish work goals. Examples of how to implement this finding are given with respect to individualized instruction, team learning and problem solving, team teaching, retaining obsolescent employees, and managerial leadership and participation in the conduct of training programs.

Guidelines are provided for the design of training systems and for the evaluation of training effectiveness.

20 *Career Development and Job Training* by James G. Stockhard. New York: Amacom, A Division of the American Management Associations, 1977.

Here is an up-to-date handbook for the design, implementation, and evaluation of employee training, education, and career development programs. The author brings a great deal of relevant experience to this task and carries it out in a practical and understandable manner.

All the elements for fashioning a variety of programs are included: the analysis of learning needs, evaluating sources of help and marshaling resources, staffing program components, selecting training and education methods, producing educational materials and training aids, conducting programs, and measuring the quality of the outcomes. Related topics focus on the allied process of career planning and organizational support.

This book may be approached from any point that is of special interest to the reader. It is intended for a general audience and not solely for training and education specialists.

21 *Matrix* by Stanley M. Davis and Paul R. Lawrence. Reading, Mass.: Addison-Wesley Publishing Co., 1977 (paperback).

The matrix organizational form is seen by many as the best way to optimize the vitality and effectiveness of organizations. Advocates feel matrix forms enhance creativity, human resource allocation, and organizational climate. It is against this background that Davis and Lawrence define the matrix form and trace its evolution. They identify the three conditions necessary for choosing a matrix design: pressures from outside the organization to make good on both complex technical demands and on the unique requirements of particular customers or clients; pressures for high information-processing capacities; and pressures upon shared resources. The response of matrix structures to these pressures is described through case studies.

The authors provide insights into the human implications of matrix organizations, including accounts of the various things that can go wrong. The special features of managing a mature organization designed along these lines are discussed. Numerous examples are provided of non-industrial applications of the matrix approach including insurance, law, banking, health care, and higher education.

22 *Visualizing Change: Model Building and the Change Process* by Gordon L. Lippitt. La Jolla, Calif.: University Associates, 1973.

This book describes the process of change that involves individual, group, and organization through the use of nonmathematical models. Since models represent the central vehicle for analysis and development in the book, the author provides the necessary background for modeling approaches as well as a description of their construction for problem solving. Actual cases provide a basis for applying the models and also permit the reader to develop some hands-on familiarity with the procedure.

Appendix II: Sample Completed Exercises for Self-Growth

Where Has Change Taken Place?

1. Personal *Ability to afford or obtain gasoline, type of car bought, limited travel, forced public transportation*
2. Family *Restructuring family activities, increased at-home leisure time, financial restrictions*
3. Social *Increase short-distance social activities, decrease general social functions*
4. Cultural *Less cultural mobility, decreased sense of cultural freedom, depressive budgeting*
5. Political *Impact increased political restrictions, public dissent, restricted free trade system, new political lessons*
6. Technological *New forms of travel, new methods of oil extraction, more efficient automobiles and oil burning*

7 Professional *New accounting procedures, govt. paperwork, increased P.R. difficulties, decreased profits*

8 Job related *Upheaval creates new positions, makes some obsolete, need for complete employee evaluation*

9 Financial *Restrictions ranging from nationwide to personal level, black market finances, illegal trade*

Impact of Change

High upset 1 → 4 Low Upset

Look over the list you made above and estimate the range of impact of each change below.

Change item	Self only	Family	Friends	Work	Employer	Own job	Other (specify)
1	1	4	4	3	4	3	
2	2	1	3	4	4	4	
3	1	1	1	3	3	3	
4	2	2	2	2	2	2	
5	2	2	2	1	1	1	
6	2	3	3	1	1	1	
7	2	3	3	1	1	1	
8	2	3	3	1	1	1	
9	1	1	1	1	1	1	

Mary Wolfe's Decision Situation

Issue: Shall I take the job of production manager? Alternatives that I have identified thus far:

1. Accept job.
2. Turn down the job but stay on with the firm.
3. Turn down the job but try to arrange a transfer to a less stressful situation.

Sample Completed Exercises for Self-Growth   225

    4 Turn down the job but start looking for other possibilities.
    5 Simply quit and develop my career elsewhere.

Put yourself in Wolfe's position and consider the five alternatives outlined above. For each alternative, list both pros and cons.

Alternatives	Pros	Cons
1 Accept	higher pay range; increased experience; company approval; ability to prove myself	possible failure; promoted beyond abilities; emotional trauma; personal difficulties
2 Turn down, stay	comfortable in old position; same subordinates; confidence in abilities	overlooked for next promotion; co. disapproval; no challenge; stagnation, obsolescence
3 Turn down, transfer	more interesting job; new location; avoid co. repercussions; new challenge, same level	undesirable transfer; unavailable transfer; inability to adapt
4 Turn down, job search	able to avoid situation; new opportunity; new challenge	new co. wary of turn down; looking for high performer at lower wage scale
5 Quit	avoid situation	unemployment; lack of funds; lack of experience

The Need to Change

To examine how this need for change works, think of a situation where you caused change to happen even though the prevailing circumstances were outwardly agreeable. It may have been a personal relationship, a job-related situation, or a change in lifestyle. It may have been getting married or getting divorced, getting fired or getting hired. Because the basic human need for change is so deeply rooted, you may not have even been fully aware of how you set up the change situation.

What was the change situation?

New manager brought in from outside the co. rather than promotion from within

First, let's deal with the conditions before change took place. Some people may have seen the situation as it was as perfectly agreeable. Others may have seen the proposed change as one actually worsening the situation. Enter these two ideas below.

1 **Situation fine the way it was**

Good system of inside promotion; good performance produces promotion

Change seen as worsening the situation

Impossible to rise regardless of performance because of use of outside sources

Second, let's recognize that a change situation can have many unfulfilling aspects although the final result is positive. Enter these two ideas below.

Sample Completed Exercises for Self-Growth   227

2   **Aspects of situation that were unfulfilling**

Feeling of lack of reward, retards motivation, higher turnover, lack of full cooperation

The final positive result

Outside manager does a better job than an inside promotion could have

Groupthink and Methink Factors in Change

To hammer the idea of methink home, consider five groups of which you are a member. These may be broad groups such as male/female or ethnic affiliation or more specific groups such as professions, community organizations, or sports fans, or vegetarians. Tell how the group as a whole would be characterized about a particular issue or event. Then describe some way in which you differ from the group opinion.

	Group	Issue or event	Groupthink	Methink
1	Drug mfg.	Bulk to private pharmacy	Pro higher profits	Beyond production capabilities
2	Airline	Reduced fares	Increased consumption	Can show long-run loss
3	Retail	New floor manager	Good dept. manager	Knowledge of employee dissatisfaction
4				
5				
6				

Helping Others to Change

DIMENSIONS OF THE TASK

METHODS	The task itself	Time span	Persons involved	Degree of change required
Focus on Circumstances				
Hat changing	Promotion to dept. mgr.	2 mos. training	Present mgr., present subordinates	Moderate
Environment changing	City to city transfer	6 mos.	Indiv.	Extensive
Messages	Fire supervisor	2 wks.	Supervisor	Extensive
Reward and punishment	Bonus	Once a year	Vice president	Minimal
Focus on Persons				
Friendship, admiration, respect	New system	1 yr.	Production mgrs.	Extensive
Training and development	Promotional push	5 yrs.	Line mgrs.	Moderate
Technical training	New machinery	6 mos.	Production mgrs.	Moderate
And Don't Forget:				
Time as a strategy				

Sample Completed Exercises for Self-Growth

Helping Others to Change (continued)

RESOURCES AND CONSTRAINTS

Resistance*	Organizational resources and constraints†	Your resources and constraints‡
Existing mgr. does not wish to take prom.	Lack of trained personnel for alternate positioning	Ability to help existing mgr. readjust
Doesn't want to leave family	Absolutely need employee's skill in new location	Lose transition
Doesn't want to leave	Reorganizing	Job search
Higher bonus minimal	Budget constraint	Additional non-monetary benefit
Used to old method, comfortable	Necessity for new method to avoid obsolescence	Encourage new capabilities, advantages
Present mgrs.	Lack of outside resource	Monetary reward
Resist effort, need for change	Profit decline	Use org. probe. and benefit for training

*Try to take account of where resistance originates: WHERE HAS CHANGE TAKEN PLACE? HOW DOES CHANGE AFFECT ME? DO I HAVE THE ABILITIES TO CHANGE? DO I WANT TO CHANGE?

†Include: climate for innovation; personnel; financial state; relationship to the larger environment

‡Include: formal authority; informal power; knowledge and skills

Planning Your Own Change Program

Steps Leading to Final Goal of Change Program

Considering these related objectives and the goal (change), what do you see as necessary steps in order to launch the process? Refer back to the Madison Plastics example for help in developing your own scheme.

(1) Establish investment financing.
(2) Bring in planning engineers to survey needs and make preliminary design plans.
(3) Estimates of needed capital investments, plant modifications, and additional necessary labor.
(4) Create prototypes of new machinery.
(5) Tests and safety measures must be performed on proposed machinery.
(6) New employees must be trained and procedural assembly-line techniques established.
(7) Production outputs and sales needs established.

Further Elaboration of Each Step in Change Process

Review each of the steps you just listed, providing additional details and comments regarding action to be taken. For example, what kinds of information might you require from a manager, what types of procedures need to be mod-

Planning Your Own Change Program (continued)

ified, and what subgoals could be set up to monitor progress? The questions below (which focus on helping others to change and gaining the support of associates) may suggest points you have not fully considered.

In arranging financing, ask managers:
1. *level of need, reliable past investors, rate of return, return logs, etc.;*
2. *engineers necessary to modify or create new models;*
3. *managers' estimates of machinery and labor necessary for the proposed change; modification in the plant also necessary.*
4. *In building prototypes, subgoals would have to be time limitation for improvements and progressive designs.*
5. *Modified test and safety measures would be necessary for the new types of machinery.*
6. *Managers could supply info as to their labor and training needs and report on learning curves and proposed production start.*
7. *Sales managers necessary to estimate output levels and the rate and progress of incoming sales.*

Where Do You Anticipate Problems in Your Master Plan?

Would one department head be ill-equipped to handle new responsibilities, for example? Could some adverse local publicity delay implementation? Do you think you could delegate considerable authority? What could you build in to offset anticipated problems?

Possible Problems	Possible Solutions
Inadequate financing	*Preestablish loan capabilities; reuse previous sources*
Training inadequate *Old employees unmodifiable* *Employee resistance* *Lack of coordination in new depts.*	*Use training procedures tried and true in comparable mfg. firms, complete org. charting, increased employee relations*
Additional trained labor unavailable	*Increase recruiting teams, scout similar mfg. co., use past files, make selection techniques more efficient to speed hiring practices.*

Evaluating Your Performance

How do you now judge your general aptitude for guiding large-scale change such as you have just outlined?

```
                          X
_____
  POOR        FAIR        OK         GOOD
```

Index

Abilities to change, 18, 56, 189, 198, 200
Age, 34–35, 157
Ambivalence, 33–34, 202
American Society of Personnel Administrators (ASPA), 185–86
Analytical methods, 44
Anticipation of changes, 50–51, 52, 122–23
Attitudes, 18–19, 170
　ambivalence in, 33–34, 202
　goals and, 64
　systems thinking and, 55, 202

Baselines for change, 14–16
Biases, 147–60, 204
Broadening horizons, 49

Change consciousness, 9
Charting techniques, 44
Circumstance changing, 42–43, 72–91, 119–20, 167, 202–3
Commitment, 84
Communication, 81–85, 87, 96, 112, 167, 169
Computer-related systems, 44
Confidence, 28–29
Conflict, 99–102
Continuing education units (CEUs), 186
Control models, 44
Costs of Organization Development, 134
CPM, 44
Credentialing, 183–92, 204

Definitions, 39, 58, 77, 83–84
Degree of impact, 11–12
Deviance, 149

Economic goals, 60, 61
Education, continuing, 186, 188–89. *See also* Training
Environment changing, 79–80
Expectations, 149–50
Experience through time, 108

Facts, 101
Fear, 28, 200
Feedback, 169
Finance of credentialing, 190
Flexibility, 62-63, 75, 170

Gantt-type charts, 44
Goals, 52, 55–67, 168–69
　organizational, 43, 57, 121, 168–69, 202
　training and, 106, 107, 113
Grandfathering, 186, 188
Groupthink, 34–35

Hat changing, 74–78, 114. *See also* Roles
Hospital admitting function, 125–26, 127–30

Idealizing the present, 30
Impact model, 11–12
Inconvenience, 29–30
Information, 81-85, 87, 96, 112, 169

Intellectual goals, 60, 61
Interrelationships,
    circumstantial, 42–43, 44, 45. See also Relationships, human
    goals and, 43, 57, 59–61, 65
    problem-related, 48

Leadership, 96–97, 112–13, 133–34, 167, 203
Legislation of change, 86–87, 183–92, 204
Lifestyle, 29–30

Magnitude of change, 121, 122, 124
Marken, 44
Mathematical models, 44
Means to goals, 71, 167, 205
    flexibility in, 62–63
    goal-preceding, 61
    and objectives, 56–57
Messages, 81–85, 87, 96, 112, 169
Methink, 34–35
Misfits, 149
Monitoring, 9, 24, 120
Motivation, 61, 106–7, 133, 200, 202
    for credentialing, 189, 191

Need for change, 32–34, 58
Novelty, 32, 82
Numbers of people, change-affected, 121–22

Objectives, 56–57, 58, 65, 166, 167
Objectivity, 40–41, 201
Obsolescence, 156–57
Organization Development (OD), 45, 98, 119–41, 167–79

Participation in administration, 152–55
Performance-based objective, 58

Person changing, 72–73, 119–20, 170
    and credentialing, 189–90
    by environment changing, 79
    time horizons for, 29, 123–24
    through training, 98–114, 132–33, 147–49, 156–57, 168, 170, 186, 188–89
Personnel credentialing, 185–89
PERT, 44
Planning, 121, 155–57, 167–68, 169
    models for, 44
    with time strategy, 108–9
Policy, organizational, 147–60, 166, 204
Power, 203
Predictability, 23–29
Prestige of administration, 152
Problem solving, 45–48, 103–4
Professionalism, 126–27, 185–92
Programming, 44
Promotions, 85
Punishments, 85, 86–87
Purchasing function, 125, 126, 127, 130–34

Reality alternatives, 48–49
Recruitment procedures, 147–50
Redefinition, 83–84
Redirection, 120–21, 170–71
Regulation, credentialing, 183–92, 204
Relationships, human
    analysis of, 44
    change-inspiring, 95–98, 112, 167
    goals with, 60, 61
    in Organization Development, 134–35, 141, 167
Resistance to change, 28–31, 34, 170, 200, 202, 205
    messages and, 83–84
    and predictability, 23, 24, 28–29
    and subgoals, 59
Respect, 96–97, 112, 150–51, 167

Rewards, 85–86, 87–88, 112
Roles, 74–78, 101, 114, 203

Self-development, 99, 200
Sensitivity, 50–51
Shock effect, 55, 82–83
Status, 29
Subgoals, 58–59, 168–69
Systems thinking, 39, 42–52, 109, 168, 201–5
 and attitudes, 55, 202
 and goals, 61, 202
 and objectivity, 41, 201

Task identification, 109
Team building, 133
Technical goals, 60, 61, 123, 167
Technical training, 105–7, 113
 with continuing education, 186, 188–89

and obsolescence, 156–57
 in Organization Development, 132–33, 168
Time
 for Organization Development, 120, 121, 123–24, 125, 129, 134, 168, 170
 personal horizons of, 29, 123–24
 schedules of, 120, 121, 123–24, 129, 168
 as strategy, 108–9
Training, 98–114, 147–49, 170
 technical, 106–8, 113, 132–33, 156–57, 168, 186, 188–89
Turnover, 150

Uncertainty, 27–29, 189

Book Order Forms

If after reading *The Manager's Guide to Change* you feel that some of your friends or colleagues should have copies, please clip out the order forms below and pass them along.

MAIL TO:

Lifetime Learning Publications
Ten Davis Drive
Belmont, California 94002

Please send me _____ copies of *The Manager's Guide to Change* at $9.95 each. I understand that if I am not satisfied, I can return the book for a complete refund within 30 days.

☐ Check enclosed   ☐ Bill my credit card account:
　　　　　　　　　　　　　　BankAmericard or Visa # _____
　　　　　　　　　　　　　　Master Charge # _____

　　　　　　　　　　　　　　_____
　　　　　　　　　　　　　　(signature)

Name _____

Address _____

City _____ State _____ Zip _____

MAIL TO:

Lifetime Learning Publications
Ten Davis Drive
Belmont, California 94002

Please send me _____ copies of *The Manager's Guide to Change* at $9.95 each. I understand that if I am not satisfied, I can return the book for a complete refund within 30 days.

☐ Check enclosed   ☐ Bill my credit card account:
　　　　　　　　　　　　　　BankAmericard or Visa # _____
　　　　　　　　　　　　　　Master Charge # _____

　　　　　　　　　　　　　　_____
　　　　　　　　　　　　　　(signature)

Name _____

Address _____

City _____ State _____ Zip _____

Book Order Forms

If after reading *The Manager's Guide to Change* you feel that some of your friends or colleagues should have copies, please clip out the order forms below and pass them along.

MAIL TO:

Lifetime Learning Publications
Ten Davis Drive
Belmont, California 94002

Please send me _____ copies of *The Manager's Guide to Change* at $9.95 each. I understand that if I am not satisfied, I can return the book for a complete refund within 30 days.

☐ Check enclosed   ☐ Bill my credit card account:
　　　　　　　　　　　　　　BankAmericard or Visa # _____
　　　　　　　　　　　　　　Master Charge # _____

_____
(signature)

Name _____

Address _____

City _____ State _____ Zip _____

MAIL TO:

Lifetime Learning Publications
Ten Davis Drive
Belmont, California 94002

Please send me _____ copies of *The Manager's Guide to Change* at $9.95 each. I understand that if I am not satisfied, I can return the book for a complete refund within 30 days.

☐ Check enclosed   ☐ Bill my credit card account:
　　　　　　　　　　　　　　BankAmericard or Visa # _____
　　　　　　　　　　　　　　Master Charge # _____

_____
(signature)

Name _____

Address _____

City _____ State _____ Zip _____